Also by JOHN BAILLIE

AND THE LIFE EVERLASTING
INVITATION TO PILGRIMAGE
A DIARY OF PRIVATE PRAYER
THE BELIEF IN PROGRESS
A DIARY OF READINGS
THE SENSE OF THE PRESENCE OF GOD

Published by Charles Scribner's Sons

OUR KNOWLEDGE OF GOD

OUR KNOWLEDGE OF GOD

By

JOHN BAILLIE

D.Litt., D.D., S.T.D.

*Professor-Emeritus of Divinity
in the University of Edinburgh*

The bird that sees a daintie bowre
Made in the tree, where she was wont to sit,
Wonders and sings, but not his power
Who made the arbour: this exceeds her wit'
But Man doth know
The spring, whence all things flow:

And yet as though he knew it not,
His knowledge winks, and lets his humours reigne:
They make his life a constant blot,
And all the bloud of God to run in vain.
Ah, wretch! what verse
Can thy strange wayes rehearse?

NEW YORK

CHARLES SCRIBNER'S SONS

231
B1570

215845

FRATRI SUO
D. M. B.
CUIUS MENTE QUASI COTE
MENTEM SUAM EXACUERE SOLET
LIBRUM HUNC QUALEMCUNQUE
D.D.D.
AUCTOR

PREFACE
TO THE EDITION OF 1959

IT is nigh on twenty years since this little book was first published and some years more since most of it was written, but the publishers tell me that it continues in steady demand, and they have very kindly asked me whether I wish to make any changes in the text for this new printing. I have, however, judged it best to leave it as it stands, adding only these few further prefatory words.

Were I now to write the whole afresh, I should naturally put things a little differently. Neither theology nor philosophy has remained static in the interval, and I should now find myself dealing with certain new-emerging challenges to my position, while at the same time being able further to clarify that position by the aid of some very enlightening contributions that have meanwhile been made.

One cannot but be aware that there is at present much less mutual understanding between the philosophers and the theologians of the English-speaking world than at any previous period. It is not so much that the two groups of practitioners arrive at contradictory conclusions—that happened often enough in the past—as that they are in less effective communication with one another than they used to be. They no longer talk the same language. Too few of our philosophers have taken pains to understand what our theologians are saying, and too few theologians to understand the philosophers; and that seems to me most regrettable. There are of course a number, perhaps an increasing number, of notable exceptions to this, but not yet enough to ensure a satisfying co-ordination of the two interests or to avert the danger of a sort of schizophrenia developing in the intellectual life of our period.

Were I now to add anything to what I have written, it would above all be to relate it to the thought, and to answer the challenge, of that philosophical trend which in its rapidly succeeding stages has answered in turn to the names of logical atomism, logical positivism, and logical or linguistic analysis; and I should be particularly addressing myself to the question now so insistently put to us: How are theological statements verified? This, however, could not easily be done in short compass, and if it is to be done at all, it must be in a separate publication. Nor is it impossible that I should contemplate such in the not very distant future.

JOHN BAILLIE

EDINBURGH, October, 1958.

PREFACE

THIS is an essay in the most difficult of all subjects. No other investigation that we ever undertake makes so heavy a demand upon our spiritual powers or requires for its successful conduct so mature and many-sided a wisdom as does our attempt to understand the relations of God to the soul, and one cannot but be conscious of one's own inadequacy in face of such a task. At the present time the field is occupied by a number of competing views, each of which is likely to have something valuable to contribute to our total understanding, yet any two of which necessarily exclude one another if accepted in the form in which alone they are offered to us by their most devoted adherents. My purpose has been the irenic one of endeavouring to distinguish the true insight within each alternative from that blindness in it which renders it insensitive to the insight of the other. My success in this endeavour has been by no means such as to satisfy me, but I hope it will be allowed that I have at least resisted the temptation of evading any of the problems into which the argument has led me, however delicately complex—because situated at what are precisely the growing-points of the thought of our time—some of these have turned out to be.

The present is not the first occasion on which I have been bold to enter this general field, and an occasional reference to my earlier appearances will be found in the footnotes of the present work. Nevertheless I should prefer that what I have now written should be allowed to stand as a whole by itself; for though my present findings may seem to myself to be for the most part a not unnatural development of my findings of twelve or fifteen years ago, I am well aware that the agreement between the two is far from complete.

Various selections from the matter here contained have formed the substance of special courses of lectures in several universities—the Gunning Lectures in the University of Edinburgh in February 1936, the Nathaniel William Taylor Lectures in Yale University in April of the same year, a course of three Special Lectures in Theology in the University of London in November and December 1937, and three lectures at the Easter School of Theology in the University of St. Andrews in March of the present year. But what I said on most of these occasions has been considerably revised; and the whole was planned before the parts were chosen from it. To the authorities who so kindly invited me to deliver the various lectures, and to the audiences which gave them so indulgent a hearing, I wish to express my cordial thanks.

Very real gratitude is also due to the Rev. J. Y. Campbell, M.A., formerly of Yale University and now of Kilmacolm, and to my brother, the Rev. Professor D. M. Baillie, D.D., of St. Andrews, who have once again helped me by reading the proofs (and the latter also by reading my manuscript) and purging my work of various disfiguring errors.

JOHN BAILLIE

EDINBURGH
May, 1939

CONTENTS

OUR KNOWLEDGE OF GOD

CHAPTER I
CONFRONTATION WITH GOD

§1

THE great fact for which all religion stands is the confrontation of the human soul with the transcendent holiness of God. When God reveals Himself to man, then a characteristic disturbance is set up in the human soul and in the life of our human society, and that disturbance is what we mean by religion. It is a disturbance of which we have all had some experience. Not one of us has been left alone by God. Not one of us has been allowed to live a purely human life with complete peace of mind. It is, indeed, our common sin and shame that we do our best to ignore God's gracious approach, shutting ourselves up within our human finitude, living unto ourselves alone, as if God were not there at all. Nevertheless, try as we may, we never quite succeed in shutting God out. We never quite attain the self-containedness we so impiously desire. We can live in forgetfulness of Him, but not with peace of mind. We can live without His blessing, but not without His judgement. 'And so,' as St. Anselm wrote more than eight hundred years ago, 'should any man or bad angel be unwilling to submit to the divine will and rule, yet he cannot escape from it; for when he would escape from under the will that commands, he does but rush under the will that punishes.'[1]

That is your experience and mine, but can we say that it has always been the experience of everybody? Are

[1] *Cur deus homo*, Bk. I, Ch. XV.

3

there any men, or have there ever been any men, whose self-sufficient finitude has never been disturbed by the approach of God at all? Are there men, or have there ever been men, in whose experience religion has played no part? Is there a consciousness which, while already fully human, is yet *merely* human, and has never been invaded by the divine?

It is clear to me that I cannot find such a consciousness by going back to the beginnings of my own experience. No matter how far back I go, no matter by what effort of memory I attempt to reach the virgin soil of childish innocence, I cannot get back to an atheistic mentality. As little can I reach a day when I was conscious of myself but not of God as I can reach a day when I was conscious of myself but not of other human beings. My earliest memories have a definitely religious atmosphere. They are already heavy with 'the numinous'. They contain as part of their substance a recognition, as vague and in-articulate as you will, yet quite unmistakable for any-thing else, of what I have now learned to call the divine as a factor in my environment. I cannot remember a time when I did not already feel, in some dim way, that I was 'not my own'[1] to do with as I pleased, but was claimed by a higher power which had authority over me. You may say that this higher power represented only my parents or my nurse. If by this you mean that that is *your* view of the source from which the claim proceeded, then I am not for the moment concerned to refute it. But if you mean that that was *my* view of the matter, then I

[1] καὶ οὐκ ἐστὲ ἑαυτῶν. I Corinthians vi. 20.

4

must dissent. For, as far back as I can remember anything, I was somehow aware that my parents lived under the same kind of authority as that which, through them, was communicated to me. I could see that my parents too behaved as though they, *even they*, were not their own; and had they behaved as though they were their own and might do what they liked and might ask of me merely what they liked to ask, their authority over me could not have had the character which I actually felt it to possess. No, with the best will in the world, I cannot say that it was the social organism to which I belonged that seemed to be claiming me. Rather was I a member of a social organism that was itself aware of a claim. Long afterwards I was introduced to the conception of a merely social morality that was entirely without numinous quality or divine reference, but I am quite sure that my infantile moral consciousness was of a very different order.

Clearly, however, my infant experience was determined for me, to an extent to which it is difficult to set a limit, by the long tradition in which I stood. I was born into a Christian home, and God's earliest disclosure of His reality to my infant soul was mediated to me by the words and deeds of my Christian parents. Had I been born into the first generation of human infants, or into a society of the most primitive kind of which we have any knowledge or record, my experience could not possibly have been what it was. But would it still have had some religious quality? One way of seeking an answer to this question is to ask, Are the most primitive human societies now known to us already aware of some such confrontation? And there seems little doubt that we must say that they are. It seems nowadays to be a matter of almost unanimous agreement among those competent to judge that neither history nor geography can show us any tribe or people which is devoid of all religious awareness. We know of no human society, however savage and backward, which does not already find itself confronted with the divine. It may be a matter of dispute whether all peoples are aware of deity as personal, or even as spiritual, being; but it is not disputed that all peoples have such an awareness of the divine as is sufficient to awaken in them what it is impossible to regard otherwise than as a typically religious response. I shall not argue this further but shall take it as a matter of general agreement. It has not always been a matter of agreement, for it was often doubted in the eighteenth century and in some part of the nineteenth. But it was not doubted by the ancients. 'All men, Greeks and barbarians alike', writes Plato, 'think that gods exist and behave as if they most certainly existed and as if no suspicion of their non-existence were possible.'[1] The Stoics insisted that the concept of divinity was one of the concepts common to all mankind—a κοινὴ ἔννοια, as they said. 'What the gods are is a matter of dispute,' says the Stoic in Cicero's treatise On the Nature of the Gods, 'but that they are is denied by nobody.'[2] And Cicero begins his treatise On Divination by declaring that, so far as he knows, there is

---

[1] *Laws*, 886*a*, 887*e*.
[2] *De nat. deor.* ii. 5. 'Quales sint, varium est; esse nemo negat.'

no nation, 'however polished and educated, or however brutal and barbarous', which does not believe that the gods, to some degree at least, make known their will to men. And what these say of the barbarians St. Paul says of the Gentiles, 'Greeks and barbarians alike'.[1] To the Christian believer, he declares, God has revealed His righteousness, but to all the Gentiles He has at least revealed His wrath. 'For what of God is knowable is clear to them; God himself has made it clear. For ever since the creation of the world his unseen attributes, his eternal power and divinity, have been plainly seen in the things he has made; so that they are without excuse; because, though knowing God, they have not glorified him as God nor given him thanks.'[2] And again, 'When Gentiles who have not the Law (i.e. the Torah) do by nature the things commanded in the Law, they are a law unto themselves, though they have no Law. They show the work of the Law written on their hearts, their conscience bearing witness and their thoughts rising up within them in accusation or defence.'[3]

'So that they are without excuse.' Little indeed do the Greeks and barbarians know of God and His holy will, but they know enough to be far better men than they are! Such is the conclusion which this missionary apostle is concerned to draw. He will preach to people who cannot plead total ignorance as an excuse for their gross and terrible sins. However, our own situation goes far beyond that in which St. Paul stood. We have to preach

[1] Romans i. 14.   [2] Romans i. 19–21.
[3] Romans ii. 14–15.

7

to pagans who have not the Law, just as he had; but we have also to preach to men and women of our own land who have been born into the Christian heritage and tradition. Many of them have been brought up from infancy in what St. Paul himself called 'the nurture and admonition of the Lord',[1] and the rest have at least been brought up in an atmosphere profoundly affected by Christian ideas. Just as I said before that there is no son of man who has never been confronted at all by the challenge of the divine, so I should say now that there is no child of the West who has not in some degree been confronted by the challenge of God in Christ. Far more, then, of our modern Western world than of that old Mediterranean world to which St. Paul first applied them, must the words be spoken, 'So that they are without excuse'. For it must be true that, as Thomas à Kempis has said, 'How much the more thou knowest, and how much the better thou understandest, so much the more grievously shalt thou therefore be judged, unless thy life be also more holy.'[2] In these Western lands the Christian gospel has been so long proclaimed that it has not only reached every ear but left some mark on every human heart. It is quite impossible for any man to live in this country to-day as if Christ had never come. That is obviously true as regards the outward circumstances of his life, from the architecture of the city in which he lives and the Sunday closing of his shop, down to the very language which he speaks (which has been so consider-

[1] Ephesians vi. 4.
[2] *Imitatio Christi*, i. 2.

8

ably fixed for him by the Authorized Version of the Bible), and the dating of even his business letters from the year of Christ's birth. But it is also true, I believe, of his most inward consciousness—and not least of what we have come to call his 'subconsciousness'. Something of the challenge of Christ has been felt by all. It is to be feared there are many who have never responded to that challenge, but are there any who have not in some degree been troubled and stung by it? There are many who live as if Christ had never come, but are there any who do so with complete peace of mind? The question may at first seem a strange one in view of the amazing smugness and self-satisfied worldliness that pervades most of our society. 'Is it nothing to you, all ye that pass by?' Often it seems to be less than nothing. Yet a closer scrutiny will, I think, enable us to see that where Christ has not been allowed to bring peace, He has at least not been prevented from bringing a sword. The surface life of our society may appear to be unruffled, but that is only because the disturbances are being forcibly held down in the interior depths of individual minds. On 18 August 1908 Thomas Hardy jotted down this in his diary: 'If all hearts were open and all desires known—as they would be if people showed their souls—how many gapings, sighings, clenched fists, knotted brows, broad grins, and red eyes would we see in the market place!'[1] Yes, the life of the market-place in Hardy's Dorchester or any other English town is far from presenting to God the same placid and genteel appearance that it wears to our unseeing eyes! Where we see only a

[1] *The Later Years of Thomas Hardy*, by F. E. Hardy, p. 133.

contented humdrum, God sees a sorry muddle and tangle, and a heap of human trouble. We must believe He sees the humour of it; and of that Thomas Hardy could see a little too. But the humour of it is lost in the pity of it; so that He covers it all with the passion of His redemptive enterprise in Christ His Son.

Moreover, the psychological discoveries of recent years have, as I believe, done us the service of enabling us to look deeper than even Hardy saw, and to distrust still more the apparently unruffled surface of an ordinary life. Our eyes have been opened to the existence of a still lower submarine depth into which the disturbances may, as the psychologists say, be 'repressed'. Not only may men's faces and their words belie their thoughts, but likewise their conscious thoughts may belie the 'subconscious' workings of their minds. And the psycho-analysts have shown us how essentially dangerous and unstable, and even explosive, this condition of repressed disturbance must always be, and how the many forms of nervous and mental sickness with which the modern world is harassed are nothing but the revenge taken upon our sham serenity by conflicts which, instead of being courageously faced and resolved, were dealt with in this evasive way.

In the light of this closer scrutiny, the world's apparent self-containedness and indifference to God's transcendent claim begin to wear a somewhat different look. I do not mean to say that the only conflicts that are repressed, and whose repression gives rise to morbid symptoms, are conflicts caused by the refusal of a divine challenge whose right we nevertheless recognize. Yet as one goes through the case-books of the psycho-analysts one is surprised to discover from how few cases of troubled mental life this spiritual element seems to be entirely absent. The ostensible causes of the inferiority complex are indeed many and varied. A recent newspaper report mentions the following amusing list: 'Being too small; being too large; being too rich; being too poor; being the son of a clergyman, a tradesman, or a nobleman; having a bodily deformity or weakness; having to wear spectacles; being deaf; having a dark skin or being of mixed race; having an awkward name, e.g. John Bull; being out of work; and old age.' But, in the first place, it is doubtful whether such a list does not omit a very important class of causes, namely those appertaining to that most inward deformity of all—the deformity of a bad conscience. And in the second place, it is difficult to believe that a merely outward deformity or disability could of itself have any such sequel where such an inward deformity was not also present. 'The sting of death is sin.'[1] It is really our sins that make our misfortunes unbearable, just as it is God's grace that can transmute them into instruments of blessing, making sweet the uses of adversity. As has been well said, 'Sin is the chief source of the bitterness and perplexity of suffering; it throws a shadow across vision, making it appear other than it is. If suffering has an insupportable sting in it, crushing and embittering the soul, it is not because it is, so to say, suffering *per se*, but because it meets and enters into an alliance with the lovelessness of man

[1] 1 Corinthians xv. 55.

11

without, and with a profound disquietude and dissatisfaction with ourselves within, a disorganized and corrupted inner life estranged and alienated from God.'[1] This is why the rest of organic nature is largely or wholly immune from the nervous tensions, the divided selfhood and the conscientious struggles that harass the human soul. Only man can never again rest happily in a purely animal or vegetable life, because only to him has come the knowledge of God. Only to him has the word been spoken, 'Ye are not your own'.

But, as we have seen, to the men of our Western lands much more than that has been spoken; and this in particular, 'For ye are bought with a price.'[2] We have to do not only with the knowledge of God, but with the knowledge of God in Christ. The celebrated psychologist Dr. C. G. Jung was recently quoted as having remarked that in his analysis of the psychoses of Jews he was constantly finding one element to be resistance to the Cross. If that surprises us in the case of those who have the established authority of a long tradition behind them in resisting Christ's Cross, how much more must it be true of those in the Christian world who, in resisting it, are going contrary to their own accepted standards!

The fact is, then, that our Western human nature is spiritually much more vulnerable than it looks. Our apparent self-sufficiency is largely on the surface and does not go deep. Beneath the superficial placidity of our modern society there is an uneasy conscience, and with

[1] H. H. Farmer, *The World and God* (1935), p. 247.
[2] 1 Corinthians vi. 20.

the creation of this uneasiness the Christian gospel has had very much to do. Other elements, of course, enter into it—elements going back to the savage mind's first awakening to a higher claim, elements proceeding from Greek and Roman and especially from Stoic sources, elements connected with the old Nordic tradition which you will find so admirably described in Tacitus's *Germania*. But the great shadow on the conscience of the modern West is the shadow of the Cross.

Now this hidden canker of an uneasy conscience is in itself our greatest scathe and scourge, and for that only our own disobedience is to blame; yet it is but the reverse side of our most precious blessing, and for that we must thank God as for nothing else that has come to us. For it means that however much we try to keep to ourselves, yet He will not leave us to ourselves. It means that He invades even our 'ultimate heart's occult abode'.[1] It means that His is a love that has claimed us from the beginning, and that to the end refuses to let us go. It means that the Hound of Heaven is still on our traces 'with unhurrying chase, And unperturbèd pace, Deliberate speed, majestic instancy'. It means that 'Fear wist not to evade as Love wist to pursue'. And therefore it is just when I am farthest from inward tranquillity, when my selfhood seems most divided, but also when the superficial tranquillity of an apparently unified selfhood is invaded by an uprush of morbid mental symptoms, and yet again (if we are to believe the psychologists) when the tranquillity of my waking life gives place at night to a ferment

[1] Francis Thompson, *A Fallen Yew*.

of distracted dreams—it is then that I must most solemnly
ask myself

> Halts by me that footfall:
> Is my gloom, after all,
> Shade of His hand, outstretched caressingly?[1]

A true understanding of this situation is of the greatest
importance, not only for the discipline of our own minds
but for the bearing of our Christian witness in the modern
world. During the last several generations we who
preach the gospel have been far too ready to assume that
the modern man had developed an immunity against its
appeal. We have approached him apologetically. We
have made stammering excuses for our intrusion. For
the old direct challenge we have substituted the language
of debate. Where our forefathers would have confronted
him with God's commandments, we have parleyed with
him over God's existence and over the authenticity of
His claims.

And now, it would seem, we are beginning to learn
our mistake. We used to hear it said, only a decade or
two ago, that the day of the old dogmatic preaching was
over. Perhaps there are still some who speak like that.
But there are many more who are beginning to wonder
whether the day of the new apologetic preaching is not,
in its turn, passing away. We are awakening to the weakness of this supposedly improved strategy, and beginning
to suspect that the old frontal attack may after all have
been better suited to the fundamental realities of the

[1] These well-known phrases are all from Francis Thompson's *The Hound
of Heaven.*

situation. It seems to me that the signs of this change of mind are everywhere about us. The two new religious or theological movements that have been most discussed during the years since the War are, I have no doubt, those associated with the names of Dr. Frank Buchman and Dr. Karl Barth respectively. Very different as these two movements are in other ways, this change of mind and method is a feature common to them both,[1] and there can be little doubt that it is to this common feature that each has owed its considerable measure of success in disturbing the complacency of this present generation. And the same thing is true far beyond the scope of these two particular movements.

Indeed, the present danger may well be that this reaction, like most others, will, before its force is spent, carry us altogether too far, so that we lose touch with reality as it were in the opposite direction. To say that there is *something* which we may take for granted is not to say that there is nothing which we must defend by argument. Apology has its uses no less than confident assumption and assertion; and apologetic no less than dogmatic. The proper area of dogmatic assertion is a very narrow one indeed; and there is little doubt that, as the tendency of the former age was to ignore it altogether, so the tendency of the present age is to extend it indefinitely in the interest of each competing conviction.

[1] We shall immediately, however, have occasion to note that, in the case of Dr. Barth himself, his rejection of apologetic seems to be based, not on his recognition of an implicit knowledge of God which requires no argument to support it, but on his denial that there is any implicit knowledge which could serve as a starting-point for argument.

This is obviously true in the political sphere, where 'we are tempted to renounce God's methods of *winning* men, and to substitute, under some such high-sounding name as the "leadership-principle", the method of putting on shirts of brown or black or blue and knocking them on the head'.[1] But, as the writer of these words is careful to point out, we are displaying the exact theological counterpart of this political strategy when we present religious truth to men in the form of 'an inscrutable revelation which they are not competent to criticise'.[2] A religion that refuses to exhibit its own reasonableness is fellow to a political régime that refuses to submit to a free referendum, and it is no accident that the two are products of the same age. We may, then, do as much damage by rudely rebuffing an honest perplexity as by solemnly reasoning with a veiled insincerity. The attitude represented by the saying, 'Never mind the mistakes of Moses, sir; where were you last night?' probably misses the reality of the case as often as it hits it. But though the proper area of assumption is a very narrow one, it nevertheless belongs to the very profoundest region of the spirit's life. The most important of all verities is a verity that cannot be argued. Into whatever contrary excesses our generation has been misled, we cannot but be thankful that it has returned to some understanding of this truth, and that in so doing its eyes have been reopened to what I have called the spiritual vulnerability of even the most apparently self-enclosed human nature.

[1] Leonard Hodgson, *Democracy and Dictatorship in the Light of the Christian Faith* (1935), p. 30.   [2] Ibid., p. 11.

§2

I HAVE already mentioned Dr. Barth and must often mention him again—nobody seems to be able to talk theology these days without mentioning him. And I propose now, at the very forefront of our discussion, to try to define the difference between the things that I have myself been saying and the well-known views which are associated with his name. This will, I hope, be a first step towards the further clarification of the position I wish to defend.

My contention has been that the only humanity known to us is a humanity which has already, in some degree at least, been confronted with the reality of God and disturbed by the challenge of His holy presence, and that it is this fact which determines the form and conditions the success alike of theological argument and of religious appeal. That not one of us has been left quite alone by God, that we have been sought out from the beginning, that from the beginning we have possessed more light than we have used—this seems to me to be a necessary part of our confession of sin. It is here, however, that Dr. Barth would emphatically disagree. It is with him a fundamental premiss that no knowledge of God exists in the world save in the hearts of regenerate Christian believers. He stands, as did Ritschl and Herrmann in previous generations, in the tradition of that Lutheran christocentrism which made Christ the Mediator no less of knowledge than of salvation; the christocentrism which denies that except in His Incarnation in Jesus of Nazareth God has ever spoken to man at all; the christocentrism which seizes eagerly on the New Testament declaration that 'neither knoweth any man the Father, save the Son, and he to whomsoever the Son will reveal him',[1] and understands that to mean that not merely God's fatherliness but His very reality was made known to men through Jesus alone. Except through revelation, he teaches, there is no knowledge of God, and there is no revelation except in Christ; 'only the man who knows about Jesus Christ knows anything at all about revelation', so that 'the confession becomes inevitable that Jesus Christ *alone* is the revelation'.[2] A younger writer of the same school goes indeed so far as to say that 'whosoever recognizes other sources of revelation besides Christ, does not belong to the Church of Christ!'[3] I do not think this excommunication need seriously trouble us, but we must at least seriously concern ourselves to disentangle the truth in such statements from the manifest error. It appears certain that

---

[1] Matthew xi. 27. Cf. Luke x. 22. 'In the original form of the saying—as attested by textual evidence in the Lukan parallel—the phrase "neither knoweth any man the Father, save the Son" appears to be lacking; it was added later to produce a formal parallelism; i.e. verse 27 ran:

> All things are shown me by the Father:
> Only He knows the nature of the Messiahship,
> And he to whom the Messiah teaches it.'

—Easton and Robbins, *The Eternal Word in the Modern World* (1937), p. 262. 'He does not say, "No man knoweth God save the Son". That would be to deny the truth of the Old Testament revelation. What He does say is that He alone has a deeper secret, the essential Fatherhood of the Sovereign Power.'—D. S. Cairns, *The Riddle of the World* (1937), p. 321.

[2] In *Revelation*, ed. Baillie and Martin (1937), pp. 48, 53.

[3] Günther Dehn, *Man and Revelation*, English translation, p. 139.

Dr. Barth is guilty of unduly simplifying the delicate complexity of the spiritual situation with which we have here to do, and that in his anxiety to recover and conserve one precious evangelic truth he is going far towards surrendering another.

What Dr. Barth expressly and unequivocally denies is that the success of Christian preaching depends even in the least degree on anything which it already finds existing in our human consciousness and to which it can address its appeal. There is, he protests, no point of contact or connexion, no *Anknüpfungspunkt*, between the Christian gospel and human nature. The gospel, when it is preached, links itself on to nothing that was there before, but rather replaces all that was there before by something totally different and altogether new. The soul of the Christian is thus in the most exact sense a creation *de novo*. Dr. Barth appeals especially to the saying of St. Paul that (as Dr. Moffatt translates it) 'there is a new creation whenever a man comes to be in Christ',[1] insisting that this expression is in no sense metaphorical but is to be understood in the most literal possible way. Conversion or regeneration, he writes, 'consists in a miracle which happens to man, a miracle on the strength of which it is no mere *façon de parler*, but a quite literal truth, that he has become a new man, a new creature'.[2] The word (*wortwörtlich*) here translated as 'literal' is probably the most emphatic word which the German language could have provided. Dr. Barth does indeed accept the doctrine that man had once been created *ad imaginem et*

---

[1] 2 Corinthians v. 17.   [2] *Nein!* (1934), p. 30.

similitudinem Dei;[1] but he holds that this image and likeness of God have been so totally defaced by the Fall as to leave not a trace behind; so that nothing but a wholly new act of creation will suffice. Man, it is true, still remains human—'he is still man and not cat', as he quaintly expresses it;[2] but his humanity has been so totally corrupted by sin that no more than a cat is he able to hear God's voice until, through faith in Christ, the image and similitude of God are created in him afresh. And with the rest of his human nature his reason also has been totally corrupted, so that since the Fall we are all, in a phrase which Dr. Barth quotes with approval from Calvin, *mente alienati,* that is to say, insane.[3] It has commonly been held that only to a rational being, such as man was supposed to be, could the knowledge of God possibly come or God's revelation of Himself be made intelligible. But Dr. Barth will not allow this; not even man's rationality can, in his view, serve as an *Anknüpfungspunkt* to which revelation can link itself. Prior to the acceptance by faith of the Christian revelation man has no capacity whatever for the reception of revelation, the capacity to receive it being given in and with the revelation itself. 'Sufficient reason for being cautious in formulating such propositions as that man and man alone possesses a nature that is able to receive God's word is', he writes, 'already to be found in the fact that the angels are clearly here left out of account, that more-

---

[1] *Vide* Genesis i. 27; v. 1. Vulgate.   [2] *Nein!,* p. 25.
[3] *Verrückt* is the word by which Dr. Barth translates Calvin's phrase. Ibid., p. 42.

over "natures" may exist of a kind unknown to us, and that we have at best no revelation but only our own guesses to go upon with regard to the receptiveness or non .eceptiveness of such unknown and non-human "natures".' And he adds that 'all man's rationality, his responsible nature and his power of decision may after all be united with utter impotence' so far as concerns the comprehension and acceptance of divine revelation.[1]

In defining our attitude to this construction I think we must begin by most cordially allowing that there is nothing in itself unacceptable, or contrary to familiar theological teaching, in the conception of a divine creative act by which both the capacity for revelation and the revelation itself are together given to creatures not hitherto endowed with either, or even with the power to think. We must not limit the omnipotence of God by saying that He *cannot* reveal His will to stocks and stones; reality is much too mysterious to us to permit of our saying that anything is impossible. Moreover, this is precisely what, at one stage of His creative work, God has quite apparently done. 'And the Lord formed man of the dust of the ground, and breathed into his nostrils the breath of life; and man became a living soul.'[2] Alike for ancient Hebrew mythology and for the most modern science, the miracle of the creation of man lies in the fact that inorganic matter did in the course of time become endowed with both the capacity and the reality of spiritual life. Furthermore, I should, as will presently appear,

[1] Ibid., p. 25. [2] Genesis ii. 7.

be the last to hold that the capacity for spiritual life was given first and the reality of it afterwards, that God first created a being to whom He could reveal Himself, and afterwards revealed Himself to that being. To make a temporal separation of this kind between the form and the matter of experience is surely quite impossible. You cannot possess the form as an empty husk prior to all filling. Man was not reasonable prior to his apprehension of the first inkling of truth, but in that apprehension his rationality was born. I find no difficulty of principle, therefore, in Dr. Barth's conception of a capacity to receive revelation which is given in and with the revelation itself.

My difficulty is not one of principle but of fact. I cannot believe that Dr. Barth's account correctly reproduces the human situation as we actually find it existing. I cannot believe that he is right in thus severing the connexion between the doctrine of the *imago dei* and the doctrine of revelation. On this view the image of God impressed upon man at creation is, as it were, a purely archaeological fact. It is something that once existed, but which has now altogether disappeared, leaving no trace upon the life of to-day. But the truth is surely that the doctrine of the *imago dei*, far from being a doctrine derived from any direct knowledge of what happened at creation, is a doctrine suggested to us by, and derived by us from, our knowledge of *present* human nature. Human nature, as we see it around us and as we know it in ourselves, is not a simple nature. Rather is it, as I have already argued, a house divided against itself. It possesses an idea of itself

which is at war with what it actually finds itself to be.
It does not present itself merely as something which is
now better than it once was—though that was how nineteenth-century progressivism and evolutionism tried to
make us conceive it. Rather is it a nature that is aware
of not living up to its own interior and acknowledged
standard; a nature whose superficial complacency was
taken by the nineteenth century at its face value and made
the basis of a philosophical theory (as by Herbert Spencer
and many others), but whose underlying inferiority com-
plexes the twentieth century has now plainly uncovered.
The doctrine of the *imago dei* has its basis in the fact that
our existent human nature presents itself to us, not as a
simply bad thing, but as *a good thing spoiled*.

Dr. Barth must not indeed be accused of treating the
imago dei as a matter of ordinary archaeology. He is well
aware of the mythical and symbolic character of the story
of the Fall. We have here to do, not with ordinary
matter-of-fact history, but with what he calls (or used to
call) *Urgeschichte*—prime history or super-history. He
knows, therefore, that it is not on the basis of any direct
knowledge of something which happened long ago that
we are able to assert that man was made in God's image
and likeness. But if it is also not on the basis of any trace
still remaining in our present human nature, then what
other basis for the assertion can we possibly have? Dr.
Barth would, I think, reply that the knowledge of the
original existence of God's image in man is a knowledge
given only to those in whose natures the image has been
re-created through Christ—and given in and with that

re-creation.[1] But I would submit that such a statement is out of accord with the known facts of the case. It is not only regenerate Christians who are aware of the essential division and doubleness of human nature, or who have experience of the conflicts to which they give rise. On the contrary, we have no knowledge of any human nature in which such doubleness and such conflict do not play a constitutive part.

Moreover, willing as we are to allow the possibility of God's revealing His will, and imparting His grace, to beings (such as stocks and stones[2]) hitherto devoid of all capacity to receive them, we are unable to feel that in His approach to us in Christ we have actually to do with such an act of omnipotence. There is miracle enough in what God does for us in Christ, but it is not a miracle of this kind. It is, in fact, not a miracle of sheer omnipotence, but *a miracle of grace*. And the exercise of grace always implies a certain self-limitation on the part of omnipotence, since there can only be grace where there is *free acceptance* in the absence of all coercion. The act of creation is an act of sheer omnipotence, but the re-creation of God's image in man is essentially an act of grace—and to that extent precisely different from an act of creation. By insisting on the literal reading of St. Paul's metaphor

[1] The dependence of Barthianism on, and its opposition to, Ritschlianism are well brought out by a comparison of Dr. Barth's teaching on this point with that of Ritschl. Cf. Ritschl, *Justification and Reconciliation*, vol. iii, English translation, p. 331: 'The doctrinal statements in the Confessions, too, regarding the original state of man, have no other significance than that of antedating the Christian ideal of life.'

[2] *Steine und Klötze*, as Brunner has it in his argument with Barth (*Natur und Gnade*, p. 18).

Dr. Barth is therefore obliterating the important theological distinction between the creative and the gracious activity of God.

When St. Paul and St. Augustine became Christians, the change that took place in them was indeed revolutionary enough and miraculous enough, yet we know well that, had God instead converted stones, or animal beings not already dowered with reason and conscience, and made good Christians and good apostles of *them*, we should be confronted with a miracle of a very different order. In spite of all that may and must be said about the radical nature of the conversion, there was clearly in the former case a continuity between what went before and what came after which there could not be in the latter. At the very least there was in the former case, as there could not be in the latter, a relevance of the remedy to the need; and this relevance is alone sufficient to indicate the essential difference between birth and rebirth, and so to afford just such an *Anknüpfungspunkt* as Dr. Barth denies. The Christian preacher to-day knows full well that his task in endeavouring to lead men to a saving knowledge of God in Christ would be a very different one were he called upon to preach to stocks and stones or to beings not already endowed with reason and some sense of distinction between good and evil and some sense of awe before the holy thing. He is indeed calling upon God to perform a miracle, but not *that* miracle—and not that miracle precisely for the reason that he is also calling upon *man* to do something, namely, to decide for God. Nobody who has ever heard a Christian preacher plead with his audience could fail to suppose that he was appealing to something that was already present in their souls.

It is therefore much more than a guess, though that (*Vermutung*) is what Dr. Barth calls it, when we say that man's already existing reason and conscience and religion condition his acceptance of the Christian gospel. An abundance of witnesses could be called to the true teaching on this point. Let me summon only three. First Père Grou, who writes that 'Everything that leaves us the free use of our reasons leaves God the free use of His grace'.[1] Second Professor Tillich, who writes that 'The demand which man receives is unconditioned, but it is not strange to him. If it were strange to his nature, it would not concern him; he could not perceive it as a demand on him. It strikes him only because it places before him, in the form of a demand, his own essence.'[2] Third Canon Lilley, who writes that 'God may create a universe *ex nihilo*, but He cannot reveal Himself *ad nihilum*. . . . We may say that apart from actual communion with God there is no worthy and complete human personality. But we must also say that apart from some incipient degree of personality there would be nothing for God to communicate with.'[3] Moreover, as regards the situation in our own home lands, the preacher knows that his task would be very different from what it actually is, were those whose souls he is attempting to awaken to a saving

[1] *L'École de Jésus Christ*, xxxiii.

[2] *Die sozialistische Entscheidung* (Potsdam, 1933), translated in *The Interpretation of History* (New York, 1936), p. 208.

[3] A. L. Lilley, *Religion and Revelation* (1932), pp. 108, 111.

knowledge of God not already imbued from youth up with many ideas and feelings of a specifically *Christian* character. They may still be in a 'state of nature' rather than in a 'state of grace', but that does not mean that God has not touched their souls at all or that they are altogether unaware of His reality and authority or even of His love. All this may appear to some so elementary as to make the detailed recital of it somewhat wearisome, yet it is necessary to insist upon it, since the denial of it is so clearly implied in Dr. Barth's representations.

'Man', Dr. Barth assures us, 'is still man and not cat.' Yet if it be true that man was first created in the image and likeness of God, the total obliteration of that image could mean only the total obliteration of his humanity. For, as Calvin says, 'the image of God extends to everything in which the nature of man surpasses that of all other species of animals'.[1]

[1] *Institutio*, I. xv, §3.

§3

MOST of the passages I have quoted from Dr. Barth have been taken from the literature of his controversy with Dr. Emil Brunner. It may therefore be conducive to further clarification if I attempt to indicate also my attitude towards Dr. Brunner's counter-position. In a general way his teaching will be found to be much more in line with what I have put forward. He, too, insists on the present reality of the *imago dei* and on its relevance to our preaching as providing a point of contact in human nature which makes possible the reception by human beings of the Christian gospel. He, too, insists that God has in some degree revealed Himself to all men, and that we neither know nor can conceive of any human nature which is not already aware of confrontation with God. 'Man', he writes, 'is only man in virtue of the claim made on him by God.'[1] 'Our specifically human existence— and we have no other—consists precisely', he writes again, 'in our hearing the Word of God. We *are* what we *hear* from God. We are *men*, and have our *existence* as men through the Word of God which addresses us and calls us into existence. . . . But that means that we do not cease to be addressed by the Word of God even when in our decision we turn away from God in our wills. In this sense there is for us no absolute hiddenness of God, but only that hiddenness in which the truth and the sig-

[1] *Das Gebot und die Ordnungen*, p. 52; English translation, *The Divine Imperative*, p. 66.

nificance for our salvation of the divine Word is hidden.'[1]
The image of God is not, therefore, totally destroyed by
the Fall. The Christian revelation, when it comes, finds
man still endowed with an intelligent and responsible
personal nature. Dr. Brunner's German speech provides
him with the opportunity of forming several expressive
compound words to denote this character. He speaks of
man's *Ansprechbarkeit* or 'addressability'; of his *Wort-
mächtigkeit*, which we might perhaps translate as 'verbi-
competence'; and of man himself as a *wortempfängliches
Wesen*, a 'word-receptive being'.[2]

This receptivity and addressability, however, constitute
only the form or empty frame of the *imago dei*, and at
this point the other side of Dr. Brunner's teaching begins
to emerge; for he now draws an absolute distinction between this form and the content which fills it. The form
of the image has been retained unimpaired, but its content has, as Dr. Barth contended, been completely lost.
The true content of responsibility is freedom; but man
since the Fall, while remaining responsible, has wholly
lost his freedom of will. The true content of rationality
is goodness; but man, while remaining rational, has
utterly lost the capacity to do, or even to desire, any good
thing. 'I teach with Barth', he writes, 'that the original
image of God is demolished, that the *iustitia originalis*
and with it the possibility of doing, or even of willing,
what counts before God as good—and so also the freedom

---

[1] *God and Man*, English translation, p. 114 f.

[2] *Natur und Gnade: Zum Gespräch mit Karl Barth* (1934), p. 18. *Ansprechbarkeit* was, however, originally Ferdinand Ebner's word; see *Das
Wort und die geistigen Realitäten*, pp. 18 ff.

of the will—is lost.'[1] 'We make here', he explains, 'a distinction of category. *Formally*, the image is not infringed upon *even in the least degree*; sinful or not, man remains a responsible subject. *Materially*, the image is *utterly* lost; man is a sinner through and through, and there is nothing about him which is not stained by sin.'[2]

Now it seems to me that Dr. Barth in his reply has no difficulty in demonstrating the untenability of such an absolute distinction between form and matter. You cannot have form without matter; still less can you, as Dr. Brunner supposes, have the *complete* form without *any* matter. The one writer is as fond of making his distinctions absolute as the other is suspicious of drawing any distinctions at all; and unfortunately neither way is the way of wisdom. Dr. Barth denies that we have any revelation, any knowledge of God, any impartation of divine grace, apart from the knowledge of Christ. Dr. Brunner contends that in some measure we have all three; and there I must agree with him rather than with his adversary. But he insists on drawing an absolute distinction between such general revelation, such formal knowledge, such 'sustaining' grace, and the special saving revelation and knowledge and grace which are through Christ alone; and that seems to me as untenable a position as it does to Dr. Barth. Dr. Barth's position seems to me untrue to the facts but clearly argued; Dr. Brunner's position seems nearer the truth but, because it is not sufficiently far advanced beyond the other, to be involved

[1] *Natur und Gnade*, p. 9 f.
[2] Ibid., p. 11. Italics mine.

in confusion and unreal compromise. For while insisting that all men have the power, even apart from Christ, to attain to some knowledge of God, Dr. Brunner yet declares that this knowledge is not of the smallest saving value. But, asks his opponent, 'with what right can Brunner affirm that a genuine knowledge of the true God, however incomplete (and what knowledge of God is not incomplete?) is nevertheless not a saving knowledge? And if in fact we know the true God from the creation, apart from Christ, apart also from the Holy Spirit, how then can we go on to say that the image is, as regards the matter of it, "utterly lost" . . .?'[1] The greater part of Dr. Barth's polemic is indeed devoted to showing that the form of which Dr. Brunner speaks is bound to pass over into matter, however resolutely he may struggle to keep the two separate; and, as I have said, there can be little doubt that he makes his point.

Dr. Brunner's assertion that the content of the divine image is *utterly* lost is, however, no more unacceptable than his complementary assertion that the form of it 'is not infringed upon *even in the least degree*'. What we are here asked to believe is that the form of rationality is still fully possessed by all men, while all have completely lost the power to do or to desire anything good. Yet it appears certain that the ravages which sin has wrought upon the content of God's image in us has in no small measure extended also to the form of it; and that our reasons have been corrupted hardly less than our desires and our wills. Here, again, modern psychology has

[1] *Nein!*, p. 19.

helped us to acknowledge our sin. It has shown us how dissociation and division of personality may be the fruit of a perversion of will; and it need hardly be said that since unity (or individuality) is the very essence of personality, the division of personality is but another name for its destruction. It has shown us also how what we think to be our reasoning is for the most part only 'rationalization'. I cannot therefore follow Dr. Brunner in his facile sundering of goodness from reasonableness. If we remained perfectly reasonable, we should also remain perfectly good. For perfect goodness and perfect reasonableness are one and the same thing. And, again, utter wickedness and utter unreasonableness are one and the same thing. It is always good to be reasonable and it is always reasonable to be good, while it is always unreasonable to be wicked. But if, on the one hand, utter wickedness is the same thing as utter unreasonableness, it is equally true, on the other hand, that all wickedness involves some degree of reasonableness—a completely unreasonable being would be as incapable of wickedness as of goodness, for he would be simply non-moral. This means that total wickedness is a self-destroying conception.

The second half of this antinomy is well understood by Dr. Brunner when he distinguishes between the form and the matter of God's image. He sees clearly that evil always has the form of goodness, that is, pretends to be good; just as error has the form of truth and pretends to be true. To that extent nothing could be more admirable than his description of sinful man as a being the form of whose nature is at war with its present filling—'a contra-personal person', as he puts it, the *quod* of whose personality is contradicted by its present *quid*.[1] But what Dr. Brunner fails to see is that this distinction ceases to have meaning in the moment that it is made absolute. He does not see that when the *quid* disappears *utterly*, the *quod* itself is no longer there. He does not see that if goodness were to cease to have *any* appeal to us, then our choice of the evil way would no longer be a *choice* at all, nor in any sense whatsoever the act of a free moral agent. The truth is that a totally corrupt being would be as incapable of sin as would a totally illogical being of fallacious argument. Evil, therefore, is essentially parasitic in nature, and not anything that exists, or could exist, in its own right, independently of God who is the Good. Evil feeds on the Good which it seeks to destroy, and in destroying it completely, would therefore destroy itself. It is thus in its very essence self-destructive. Hence total corruption is not anything that can exist but is, as has been said, a limiting conception which can be approached only asymptotically. The limit, never reached in reality, is represented mythologically in the figure of the devil who, be it well noted, is no independent power but a fallen angel—and, moreover, an angel who still acts by God's permission, if not in His commission.

Indeed it would appear that there is nobody who knows better that man is not totally corrupt than does the devil himself. For otherwise why is it that he takes such elaborate care, when about to seduce us, to deck himself out as an angel of light? None better than he

[1] *Natur und Gnade*, p. 11.

understands the truth of the principle that *quidquid petitur, petitur sub specie boni.* 'Whenever I am about to commit any folly,' says Bucklaw in Scott's *Bride of Lammermoor,* 'he (the devil) persuades me that it is the most necessary, gallant, gentleman-like thing on earth, and I am up to saddle-girths in the bog before I see that the ground is soft.' Yes, that is His Infernal Majesty's invariable strategy! Yet, if we were really all devils like himself, desiring nothing that was good but delighting in evil for evil's sake, it would appear that such strategy could do nothing but defeat his purpose. And here, as it seems to me, is the clinching consideration of this whole debate.[1]

[1] It is instructive to set such a recrudescence of the doctrine of total corruption as we find in Dr. Barth in contrast with the fine equipoise of the late Baron von Hügel's teaching that not even the souls of the damned in hell are totally corrupt or 'entirely malign' (*The Mystical Element of Religion,* 2nd edition, vol. i, p. 282; *Eternal Life,* p. 390). This was something he had learned especially from his favourite St. Catherine of Genoa, who wrote that 'when we shall have departed from this life in a state of sin, God will withdraw from us His goodness, and will leave us to ourselves, and yet not altogether: since He wills that in every place His goodness shall be found and not His justice alone. And if a creature could be found that did not, to some degree, participate in the divine goodness, that creature would be, one might say, as malignant as God is good'—which would be to deny the sole absoluteness of God (*The Mystical Element of Religion,* vol. i, p. 283).

§4

IT will have been noticed that the distinction on which Dr. Brunner relies is not that between natural and revealed knowledge, but rather that between two varieties of revealed knowledge, general and special. Though the advantage of this change seems afterwards to be partly lost to him through the fact of his imparting no less a degree of rigidity to the new distinction than the scholastics were wont to attribute to the old one, the gain is nevertheless very great. For it enables him to follow Dr. Barth in denying that there can be any knowledge of God which God Himself does not impart, while affirming against Dr. Barth that all men have some knowledge of Him.

It is clear that, as soon as what used to be called natural knowledge comes in this way to be spoken of as general revelation, the traditional distinction between nature and revelation is thereby traversed and can now no longer be regarded as an absolute cleft. This result is a remarkable one and it will be well worth our while to notice carefully how it has been brought about. Prior to the nineteenth century there was no distinction that seemed simpler or more clear-cut than this one, and any child could have told you what it meant. He would have explained to you that at creation God had endowed man with the power of reason, and that by the 'unaided' exercise of this reason man had been able to find out some things about God; but that, at a later time, God had added to the knowledge thus at man's disposal by communicating to him certain further information which he could not possibly have found out for himself. Just as there are two ways of becoming possessed of the answer to a mathematical problem—by working out the problem for oneself and by being told the answer by somebody else; so it seemed to almost everybody for almost a thousand years that there were two quite distinct avenues to the knowledge of God.

But what has now happened is this. Our conception of revelation has undergone a profound change, our conception of nature has undergone what is perhaps an even more profound change; and these two changes have been of such a kind as to result in a remarkable approximation or *rapprochement* of the two kinds of knowledge. Our present view of revelation and our present view of nature are such that the distinction between them is no longer the delightfully clear and easily statable thing it used to be.

As for our changed view of revelation, there are some words of Dr. Temple, the Archbishop of York, that will serve admirably to put it before us. '*What is offered*', he writes, '*to man's apprehension in any specific Revelation is not truth concerning God but the living God Himself.*'[1] '*There is no such thing*', he writes on another page, '*as revealed truth. There are truths of revelation, that is to say, propositions which express the results of correct thinking concerning revelation; but they are not themselves directly revealed.*'[2] On this

---

[1] *Nature, Man and God*, p. 322.
[2] Ibid., p. 317. The italics in both passages are Dr. Temple's own.

view, then, revelation consists neither in the dictation of writings nor in the communication of information, but in personal communion—the self-disclosure of a Personality.[1] So also in the sphere of morals, what has been revealed to us is not a code of rules which we must obey but a Person to whom we are constrained to respond. The contrast between the two views will be sufficiently clear if we remind ourselves, for example, of the declaration of Leo XIII, in his Encyclical *Providentissimus Deus* of 1893, that the Holy Scriptures were written *dictante Spiritu Sancto*, 'at the dictation of the Holy Ghost'; or of the teaching of the Westminster Confession of Faith that 'it pleased the Lord, at sundry times, and in divers manners, to reveal himself and to declare his will unto his Church; and afterwards, for the better preserving and propagating of the truth . . . to commit the same wholly unto writing . . .', and that 'The Old Testament in Hebrew, . . . and the New Testament in Greek, . . . being immediately inspired by God, and by his singular care and providence kept pure in all ages, are therefore authentical.'[2]

But, influential as has been this changed view of revelation towards the breakdown of the old clean-cut distinction between natural and revealed knowledge, the really crucial influence seems to have been exercised rather by our changed view of nature. This is shown by the fact that, instead of the conception of revelation being

[1] Cf. the section entitled 'From Communication to Communion' in my book, *The Place of Jesus Christ in Modern Christianity*.
[2] Ch. I, §§ 1, 8.

swallowed up by that of nature, what has actually happened is rather (as we have seen) that the conception of nature has been swallowed up by that of revelation; revelation, that is, has not come to be regarded as a more special kind of nature, but nature has come to be regarded as a more general kind of revelation.

Our changed view of human nature must therefore be described somewhat more fully than was necessary with our changed view of revelation. The older psychology was wont to regard human nature as a fixed endowment which God had conferred on man at creation and which he had carried about with him ever since. This human nature consisted of various 'faculties', such as reason, conscience, a free will, and perhaps something like a religious 'instinct' or 'sense' or other innate faculty of a specifically religious kind. When this 'faculty psychology' was in its heyday, these were regarded as *separate* endowments, any one of which could have been conferred without the others; but even when it was realized that they were no more than distinguishable aspects or exercises of a single endowment, they were still regarded as fixed, innate quantities. Human nature was not the product of history but its producer; it was the precondition of history, but itself had no history. It had been bestowed ready-made upon the first man, and from him had been handed down 'by ordinary generation' to the men of to-day. Less than fifty years ago the Professor of Moral Philosophy in the University of Edinburgh was in the habit of eloquently assuring his class that 'conscience cannot be educated' but had run on the same even, reliable keel since the foundation of the world, and would continue so to do until its final dissolution.

It is readily understandable that, so long as such a view was followed, a clean-cut distinction should continue to be drawn between the light of nature and the light of revelation. Revelation stood for some kind of *present* impact of the Spirit of God on the spirit of man. But the natural knowledge of God required no such present impact; it was something that could go on, as it were, while God stood aside from its process. Human nature was, as it were, a machine which God had once created long ago, leaving it a finished article that would now run on under its own steam—though not, to be sure, without His continuing to supply it with the oil of a merely 'sustaining' grace. Such moral and religious knowledge as is to be found among men generally throughout the world is therefore not the fruit of any living experience of God's presence or any living communion with Him, but has been obtained by what was always referred to as the 'unaided' exercise of God-given powers of mind and heart.

Now, as over against such a view, many of us to-day would be almost prepared to defend the thesis that there is no such thing as human nature. Or, less paradoxically, we might say, as the Greeks would have said, that it exists, not in a state of being, but in a state of becoming. Once it was looked upon as something original and innate, but we have now come to realize that it too has had a history. We used to think of it as something that

39

God had turned out of a mould very long ago; we think of it now rather as something that is still plastic in His hands. Nature, therefore, is not really so natural as it looks. Perhaps the earliest modern to be suspicious of the old doctrine in this matter, as in so many others, was Blaise Pascal, who, having quoted the proverb *La coutume est une seconde nature*, goes on to make this comment upon it: '*J'ai grand' peur que cette nature ne soit elle-même qu'une première coutume.*'[1] But since Pascal's day many fresh lines of reflection have converged to teach us the same lesson. I recently read the phrase: 'that corrupt system of conditioned reflexes known to the bourgeois as human nature.' The words will serve to remind us of the many-sided psychological development which has culminated in the experiments of the late Professor Pavlov of Leningrad. Pavlov's conclusions have, it is true, been much drawn into the service of a completely unspiritual and merely 'behaviouristic' outlook; yet in themselves they are equally open to a religious interpretation, leaving us free to believe that, so far as there is in our corrupt natures anything of good, the 'conditioned stimulus' has in this case been the presence of the living God.

The conception of human nature was invented by Zeno of Citium, the founder of the Stoic school, who wrote a book about it entitled Περὶ ἀνθρώπου φύσεως. His teaching was that the soul of man was a detached part (μέρος καὶ ἀπόσπασμα) of the Divine Nature dwelling within the human body. It therefore contained as

[1] *Pensées*, ed. Brunschvicg, ii. 93.

part of its substance certain innate ideas (ἔμφυτοι ἔννοιαι) which were accordingly common (κοιναί) to all human beings; and among these common innate ideas were our fundamental moral notions and also our fundamental religious notions, including the idea of God. For the sum of our innate moral ideas Zeno invented the term συνείδησις, which was literally translated into Latin as *conscientia*. In this way he was the originator, not only of the conception of human nature, but also of the closely related conception of conscience; and it is hardly possible to exaggerate the influence which his way of regarding these things has had upon the thought of succeeding ages. That Zeno was right in affirming the universality of belief in God and of what he called conscience I have already been at pains to affirm. But surely he was wrong in regarding either of these as *natural* in the sense of *innate*. They *look* natural, but actually they are the fruits of a long tradition. They are not, strictly speaking, innate either in the race or in the individual, but have resulted rather from the continuing living communion between God's Spirit and the spirit of man. And, as I have already sufficiently argued, our modern Western 'conscience', and again such diffused religious ideas as seem now to be almost part of the Western mind, are in no small measure deposits left by the Christian religion itself in the course of its long progress through the generations of European history.

The truth is that there is in man no *nature* apart from *revelation*. Human nature is constituted by the self-disclosure to this poor dust of the Spirit of the living God.

This is the insight that lies behind Dr. Brunner's substitution of the idea of general revelation for that of a merely natural knowledge of God. 'Man has spirit', he writes, 'only in that he is addressed by God. . . . Therefore the human self is nothing which exists in its own right, no property of man, but a relation to a divine Thou.'[1] 'The essential being of man as man . . . is identical with his relation to God.'[2] 'The humanity of man rests in nothing else than the divine Word addressed to him.'[3] That is why humanism, when divorced from living religion, has more and more tended to debouch into mere nihilism, or into a sub-human naturalism. 'Where there is no God', M. Berdyaev wrote in his remarkable essay on *The End of our Time*, 'there is no man.'[4] 'Man without God is no longer man.'[5] And therefore, 'humanism's turning against man is the tragedy of modern times';[6] a movement of thought that 'began with the affirmation of man's creative individuality' having 'ended with its denial'.[7] The progress of modern thought seems every day to be making it clearer that between religion and naturalism there is no final resting-place in humanism. As regards anything we are *in ourselves* naturalism is true, and 'a man hath no pre-eminence above a beast'.[8] When man ceases to be rooted in God, he relapses inevitably into the sub-human.

Our conclusion must therefore be that such moral and

---

[1] *God and Man*, English translation, p. 155.
[2] Ibid., p. 157.   [3] Ibid., p. 160.
[4] Op. cit., English translation, p. 80.
[5] Ibid., p. 54.   [6] Ibid., p. 60.
[7] Ibid., p. 54.   [8] Ecclesiastes iii. 19.

spiritual knowledge as may in any one period of human history seem to have become an inherent part of human nature, and so to be an 'unaided' natural knowledge, is actually the blessed fruit of God's personal and historical dealings with man's soul, and so in the last resort also a revealed knowledge.

CHAPTER II
WAYS OF BELIEVING

§ 5

THE foregoing chapter was concerned to defend the view, as put forward by St. Paul in the Epistle to the Romans, that all men 'are without excuse; because, though knowing God, they have not glorified him as God nor given him thanks'. It may be felt, however, that in one important respect our defence still lacks completeness. We have indeed been able to show that we cannot reach a time when we did not 'know God' by going back to the beginnings either of our individual or of our racial consciousness. But some would hold that what cannot thus be found at the beginning of development may nevertheless be found at the end of it. Are there not some men, and some groups, who have *outgrown* all religion and belief in God?

In his celebrated essay *Of Atheism*, Francis Bacon asserts that 'atheism is rather in the lip than in the heart of man'.[1] That it is not in his heart I have already contended; but I think we must allow that it is not only in his lip but sometimes also in his head. There are undoubtedly some men among us who not only say but also think that they are utterly devoid of all religious belief and feeling, including belief in God. Such atheism made its first appearance in ancient Greece, in the early part of the fourth century B.C., within what has come to be distinguished by historians as the second generation of the Sophists. Plato, whom I quoted in

[1] *Essays*, xvi.

47

the foregoing chapter as observing that all known races believe in God, in the same context very clearly reveals his awareness that in the atheism of these Sophistic teachers he has to deal with what is virtually a new phenomenon in the world. He presents us with the following very significant dialogue, taking place in the island of Crete between Cleinias, a native of the island, and an Athenian tourist—who is obviously Plato himself. The Athenian has been telling Cleinias about the new Athenian atheism, Cleinias has been showing considerable incredulity, and then the dialogue proceeds as follows:

'*The Athenian*: I am afraid, my dear sir, though I will not say I am ashamed, lest these knaves will hold us in contempt. For you do not understand the cause of their being at variance with us, but imagine that their souls are urged towards an irreligious life by a lack of self-control in the matter of pleasures and desires.

'*Cleinias*: But, stranger, what other cause can there possibly be?

'*The Athenian*: One which you who live elsewhere could hardly guess; for it would be quite hidden from you.

'*Cleinias*: To what are you referring?

'*The Athenian*: To a certain very grievous sort of ignorance, which nevertheless wears the appearance of being the greatest wisdom.'[1]

This intellectual denial of the reality of God, which was so new and surprising to the Cretan, is nowadays

[1] *Laws*, 886a, b.

a variety of opinion with which, unfortunately, we are all only too familiar. True, it is not so easy as might be supposed to find examples of pure atheism. Atheism has, in fact, been not so much a term which men have used to describe their own opinions as one which has been used against them by their adversaries—used in the heat of debate, without great deliberation, and nearly always inaccurately. Socrates was charged with being an atheist. The Greeks in Alexandria accused the Jews of atheism, and the Jews, not content with rebutting the accusation (as we find Josephus doing), repeated it against the Greeks. St. Paul the Christian speaks of the Gentiles as ἄθεοι ἐν τῷ κόσμῳ—'without God in the world';[1] but before long the Gentiles were speaking in the same way about the Christians. Before the end of the first Christian century, Domitian put Titus Flavius Clemens to death and banished his wife, and, writes the Roman historian Dio Cassius, 'The charge against both was atheism, under which many others also were condemned as having run after the customs of the Jews.'[2] We know also that 'To the lions with the atheists!' was one of the cries raised by the populace against the Christian martyrs in the Roman amphitheatre. And in a much later day, was not even John Knox known to his enemies as 'the atheist', and so also Spinoza—though Novalis, who admired him, preferred to call him 'the God-intoxicated'?

Nevertheless there have been and are some men who

---

[1] Ephesians ii. 12.
[2] *Epitome*, lxvii. 4; quoted by B. J. Kidd, *A History of the Church to A.D. 461*, vol. i, p. 72.

would apply the term to themselves and would do so, as we must believe, with some real meaning. There are men who think they do not believe in God. I need mention only the communist leaders in present-day Russia.

The question then arises whether men may be mistaken concerning their own beliefs. Is it possible to hold that those who think they do not believe in God really do believe in Him?

The question has been investigated in an essay which I, in common with many others, have regarded ever since I first read it as one of the most important theological documents of our time—I mean the paper on 'Rational Grounds of Belief in God' which was read by the late Professor Cook Wilson to an Oxford society in the year 1897, and which has now been published in the second of the two posthumous volumes of his lectures. Cook Wilson answers the question with a confident affirmative. He is able to produce many examples of knowledge which men have possessed without being aware that they possessed it, and even while expressly denying their possession of it—cases in which 'it is not merely that we have not become aware of a necessary element in our thinking, but we have actually denied that we have it at all'. He therefore concludes that the fact that some people 'think they have no direct experience or knowledge of God' is quite compatible with the hypothesis of 'His direct presence in their consciousness'. 'The true business of philosophy', he submits, 'is to bring the belief to a consciousness of itself.'[1]

---

[1] *Statement and Inference* (1926), vol. ii, pp. 857, 858, 851.

What we have here to do with is thus a special case of the familiar distinction between consciousness and self-consciousness. All belief must in some sense be conscious—unconscious beings cannot entertain beliefs—but not all belief need be conscious of itself. We may have an awareness of a certain reality without being aware of that awareness. And we may therefore, without ceasing to be aware of such a reality, set about doubting and denying its existence—and that in all good faith. There have been people, so-called solipsists, who denied the existence of everything and everybody except their own selves. But are we, who believe in the existence of other selves, therefore obliged to allow that these other selves are not really and directly present to the consciousness of the solipsists? There have been other people, so-called subjective idealists, who denied the independent existence of the external world. But are we others, who believe in an external world which is objectively presented to our consciousness, therefore obliged to allow that it is *not* so presented to the consciousness of subjective idealists? We should not dream of allowing these things. Why then should we, who believe in God, think it necessary to allow that because some men, the so-called atheists, deny the existence of God, God cannot therefore be directly present to their consciousness as He is to ours? We should say that the solipsists and subjective idealists are as conscious of their neighbours and of the world about them as we are, but that they have been misled by false and confused philosophical argumentation into a meaningless (though doubtless quite sincere) intellectual denial of their existence. We should say that though they deny the reality of their neighbours and of the world about them with *the top of their minds*, they believe in them all the time in the bottom of their hearts. Why then should we be precluded from occupying the same ground with regard to the so-called atheists? There have even—and this, unlike the others which I have mentioned, is one of Cook Wilson's examples—been people like Hume who denied the reality of their own selves. Here the situation is more complicated, since we have now to do, not with a distinction between consciousness and self-consciousness, but with a distinction (such as Mr. J. W. Dunne has familiarized us with in his book *A Serial Universe*) between self-consciousness of the first dimension and self-consciousness of the second dimension; not with a consciousness which is not self-conscious but with a self-consciousness which is not, if we may be allowed so to express it, self-self-conscious. For we who do believe in the reality of our own selves would not only refuse to allow that Hume's self was not real; we should also refuse to allow that Hume was not conscious of its reality; the most we would allow being that he was not conscious of being conscious of it—that he had argued himself into an intellectual denial of a self-consciousness which actually was every whit as fully developed in him as it is in the rest of us.

It may possibly be objected that the case of the atheists is not entirely parallel to that of the solipsists and subjective idealists or of sceptics like Hume, in that these do not deny their acquaintance with the experiences which we others interpret as involving the direct presence of our fellow men and the external world, or of our own self-hood, but only deny the correctness of the ordinary interpretations of them. I should hold, however, that exactly the same thing is true of the atheistical denial of the direct presence of God. The Christian believer may indeed often be found pointing to experiences which he claims to have had and which the unbeliever can truly say that he has never had; but I am sure the commoner case is that the believer finds *God* in experiences which the unbeliever would equally claim to have had, but which seem to him susceptible of a purely humanistic or naturalistic interpretation. The believer finds in the most familiar experiences of life a meaning and a presence which the unbeliever does not find in them; and it is on this basis alone that he is able to proceed to those further experiences which the unbeliever cannot have at all. In the closing pages of his essay Cook Wilson provides a detailed demonstration of this fact and offers, as against the unbeliever, his own believing analysis of certain experiences which are equally familiar to both. To this point we shall have ourselves to return.[1]

[1] See p. 69 and § 20 below.

§ 6

BUT if all men have some knowledge of God and do in some sense believe in Him in the bottom of their hearts, what is it that prompts some of them to deny Him 'with the top of their minds'?

It will be remembered that the Cretan thought that men could be prompted to such a denial 'only by a lack of self-control in the matter of pleasures and desires'. St. Paul's explanation of why, 'though knowing God, they have not glorified him as God nor given him thanks', seems very much the same. Is it the true explanation?

The question can be answered only by a very honest self-examination. Every man must answer for himself. And though there may be few of us who have ever denied God's reality outright, yet there must be many of us who have experienced from within something of the nature of this doubt. Must I then say that such doubts as I have had about God have had what would usually be called a moral root? Is it because I did not relish God's commandments that I was tempted to deny His being? In my doubt of Him I seemed to be carried 'whither the argument led me', with no desire to disbelieve, perhaps even with an eager desire to believe. But was this really so?

It is well known how greatly our efforts at self-analysis have recently been aided by the remarkable researches of Dr. Freud and his followers. It has been convincingly demonstrated to us that our thinking, even when appearing to be quite straightforward, is determined by our desires in far larger measure than we had previously been in the habit of supposing. It is indeed true that this demonstration, which gave to our nineteenth-century humanism so unpleasant a jolt and is even held by many to have given it its final quietus, would have held little surprise for our more realistically minded forefathers. If Dr. Freud seems to be saying that we are all more or less insane (as indeed it was said long ago, *sed semel insanivimus omnes*), so also we have already found Calvin declaring the corruption of our reasonable natures by our sinful propensities to be so great that, ever since the Fall, we human beings are *mente alienati*. Nevertheless Dr. Freud has revealed the mechanism of this corrupting process in an entirely original way. He has explained to us in detail how we banish our less reasonable and reputable desires from self-consciousness, and 'repress' them into a subliminal region of the mind, in order that they may escape detection and that our thinking, which is really the belated 'rationalization' of conclusions to which we have already been led by our desires, may accordingly wear the appearance of straightforward reasoning toward a conclusion that was in no wise predetermined.

Must I then say that my own doubts were of this kind? I fear they were, in very real degree. Part of the reason why I could not find God was that there is that in God which I did not wish to find. Part of the reason why I could not (or thought I could not) hear Him speak was that He was saying some things to me which I did not wish to hear. There was a side of the divine reality which was unwelcome to me, and some divine commandments the obligatoriness of which I was most loath to acknowledge. And the reason why I was loath to acknowledge them was that I found them too disquieting and upsetting, involving for their proper obedience a degree of courage and self-denial and a resolute reorientation of outlook and revision of programme such as I was not altogether prepared to face. There was indeed another side of the divine reality which I was most eager to discover, and I was much distressed and perturbed in my mind because it was not revealed to me more unmistakably than seemed to be the case. For some of what God would say to me I had a very ready ear, and I was therefore greatly disquieted by my doubts as to whether He was really addressing me at all. But because there were other of His words to which I turned a deaf ear, my deafness seemed to extend even to that for which I was most eagerly listening.

It seems to me that this is very commonly the case. There has perhaps never been a man who has desired with his whole heart the non-existence of God. On the contrary, nearly all men desire His existence, though some, who have 'with the top of their minds' persuaded themselves that He does not exist, try to face the dreadful prospect bravely. We seek God 'carefully with tears'. But because we are so loath to find Him as He is, sometimes we cannot find Him at all. We have conceived our own idea of God, but it is an idea in the formation of which our sloth and selfishness have played their part;

and because there is no God corresponding to our idea, and because we are looking for none other, we fail to find the God who really is there. 'He is Thy best servant', cries St. Augustine in his *Confessions*, 'who looks not so much to hear that from Thee which is conformable to his own will, as rather to conform his will to whatsoever he heareth from Thee.'[1] It cannot be denied then that our failure to hear from God what we are most eager to hear from Him finds the greater part of its explanation in the fact that along with this which we would gladly hear He is saying certain other things to which we dare not listen. When we turn a deaf ear to His commandments, we cease also to hear His promises. We cannot be assured of His care if we reject His claim. Before religion can be known as a sweet communion, it must first be known as an answered summons. '*If* any man hear my voice, and open the door, I will come in to him, and will sup with him, and he with me.'[2] But it is futile to expect God's reality to become any clearer to us so long as we continue to shut our eyes to those aspects of His reality that are already quite plainly before us, making difficult demands upon our lives.

But is *all* our doubt of God to be explained in this way? Or is part of it of quite another kind? Are we sometimes led to doubt God's reality by thinking which, however mistaken, is nevertheless quite honest, and which, though crooked intellectually, is straightforward enough morally?

Plato would answer this latter question in the affirmative.

[1] x. 26.   [2] Revelation iii. 20.

Against the Cretan's view that all doubt of God is due to 'lack of self-control in the matter of pleasures and desires', he insists that in the Athens of the Sophistic period it was often due rather to ignorance—to 'a certain very grievous kind of ignorance, which nevertheless has the appearance of being the greatest wisdom'. In other words, doubt may sometimes spring, not from the corruption of sin, but from the limitations of finitude. It is difficult to find any corresponding admission in St. Paul. He does indeed speak, in language very like Plato's, of men who 'have become futile in their reasonings (Διαλο-γισμοῖς), till their unintelligent (ἀσύνετος) mind grew dark; though claiming to be wise, they became fools'.[1] But the context makes it quite clear that he holds such intellectual aberration to be morally conditioned. 'Honest doubt' of God was apparently as absent from the society known to Paul the Jew as it was from the society known to Plato's Cretan. Yet there can be no question that Plato was right in supposing that something of the sort, even if it existed nowhere else in the world, did exist in his own Athens. Nor can there be any question that, as a heritage from Athens, it exists in our own society to-day.

Such a conclusion is indeed demanded of us by Christian principle itself. However suspicious we ought to be of the honesty of our own doubts, we have no right to judge our neighbour's. We must remember the injunction, 'Judge not, that ye be not judged'.[2] And in particular there are two contrasted sayings of our Lord which may guide us at this point. 'He that is not against

[1] Romans i. 21-2.   [2] Matthew vii. 1.

us is for us.'¹ 'He that is not with me is against me.'²
Speaking of the latter saying in contrast with the former,
Dr. Montefiore comments as follows: 'Here a test is
given by which a man is to test himself. If he is not for
Jesus, he is against him. Before, a test was given by which
the disciples are to try others: if they are not against
Jesus, they are to be considered as for him.'³ When
applied to our present problem, this would mean that it
is well for us, as a general rule, to assume the conscientious
nature of our neighbour's doubt and to suspect the conscientious nature of our own. Such a procedure will
usually bring us out right, because in each case the rule
acts as a corrective of the error to which we are naturally
prone. But it is rather a rule of thumb than an ultimately
valid principle. There are cases in which men may do
themselves a serious spiritual injury by casting too per-
sistent and wholesale a suspicion upon the probity of
their own thinking; just as there are cases in which men
may do their neighbours an injury by taking too seriously
opinions which have no deep root in conscience and life.
What seems certain is that neither in this nor in any other
region is it permissible that we should treat the conscientious objector as an ordinary offender.

How then are we to account for such honest doubt or
denial of God's reality? The answer is perhaps twofold.
First, there is the circumstance that our conviction of the
reality of God first forms itself in our minds in close

¹ Luke ix. 50. Cf. Mark ix. 40.
² Luke xi. 23; Matthew xii. 30.
³ *The Synoptic Gospels*, 2nd edition, vol. ii, p. 194.

association with a wide context of other beliefs. In the course of our later intellectual development, however, many of these other beliefs are seen by us to be false and are quite rightly surrendered. The effort of dissociation that is then required in order to separate our deep-seated belief in God from that part of its original context which we have now been forced to reject, is an effort to which our mental powers are not always equal, so that we are faced with the difficult alternative of either keeping our belief in God and keeping with it certain other beliefs the falsity of which seems quite obvious to us, or else surrendering these false beliefs and surrendering with them our belief in God also. The dilemma, no doubt, is sometimes solved in the one way and sometimes in the other. Secondly, however, we must consider the appeal of arguments that are directed, not against the original context of our belief in God, but against that belief itself. In ancient Greece, and again in western Europe since the Renaissance, but especially in the nineteenth century, there have been current a number of philosophical outlooks which found their starting-point elsewhere than in belief in God—that is to say either in external nature or in man. These naturalistic and humanistic philosophies have not only been often very skilfully constructed, drawing into their service many of the acutest minds of the two periods I have mentioned, but they have also succeeded in persuading us of the truth and importance of some of the positions for which they have contended. But, not having set out from the reality of God, not only have they (as indeed we should have expected) failed to arrive at any conviction of His reality, but they have conducted us towards a conception of universal being from which God seems to be definitely excluded. Many men of our time are therefore in the position that, while they do (as I should contend) believe in God in the bottom of their hearts, they cannot think how to answer the arguments which certain prevailing philosophies direct against His reality, and are thus led to doubt Him 'with the top of their minds'. 'It is true', as Francis Bacon held, 'that a little philosophy inclineth man's mind to atheism.'[1]

[1] *Essays*, xvi.

§ 7

THE question may now be raised: If men may believe in God without knowing that they believe in Him, is it then very important that they should know that they believe in Him? If men may have knowledge of Him in the bottom of their hearts while denying Him 'with the top of their minds', does such denial then very seriously affect their spiritual life?

I think we must begin by very willingly allowing that the intellectual denial of God's existence need not at once completely destroy the spiritual life. Just as the intellectual affirmation of God's existence is not of itself sufficient to initiate the soul's communion with God, so the corresponding denial is not of itself sufficient to destroy that communion. After all, the central thing in religion is not our hold on God but God's hold on us; not our choosing Him but His choosing us; not that we should know Him but that we should be known of Him. And it would seem that sometimes, even when we deny Him both with our lips and with our minds, He still retains His gracious hold upon us, dwelling within us as it were incognito and continuing to do His work in and for our souls. Some of us would have to confess that even within the circle of our own acquaintance there are professed unbelievers whom we must acknowledge to be, in some very real sense, better Christians than we are ourselves. Of such men we are often inclined to say that though they cannot themselves see God at work in their souls and in their deeds, yet *we* can see Him there; that though they do not feel their conduct to be motivated by the love of God, yet *we* feel it to be so motivated. And we are accordingly forced to consider whether their denial of God does not in the last resort arise from a kind of misunderstanding: it is not so much that they have no experience of Him whom we mean when we speak of God as that, being misled by this or that humanistic or naturalistic philosophy, they speak and think of their experience in a way that seems to us to do violence to its real nature. We have, moreover, excellent authority for supposing that the children of the Most High are known much more by their fruits than by their opinions, and for arguing that 'a corrupt tree cannot bring forth good fruit'.[1] No doubt this principle may be more safely used for the generous estimation of our doubting neighbours than for the consolation of our doubting selves, and yet even this latter use must not be ruled out as illegitimate. Many a puzzled seeker has been cheered by the assurance that 'he that loveth his brother abideth in the light, and there is none occasion of stumbling in him'.[2] Yet this must not be taken to mean that love can exist without faith, or that a man can truly love his brother except God be in him. Nor again must it be taken to mean that God can be in us without imparting to us the gift of faith in Himself; for not only is the conception of a Real Presence of God apart from faith contrary to the tradition of our fathers, but it may safely be laid down that nobody who understands at all what is meant by the presence of God

---

[1] Matthew vii. 18–20.   [2] I John ii. 10.

could suppose that God could be present to a soul that had no kind of knowledge of His presence—though of course such a soul would still, like all souls, and like the beasts of the field, and like the eternal hills, be present to Him. The solution can lie only in making a distinction between different kinds of knowledge, and in holding, as I have been concerned to do, that there is a knowledge of God and a faith in Him which, being more deep-seated than any opinion, may to some extent coexist even with the opinion that we have no knowledge of His existence and no faith in His power to save.

I think it is to be noted also that when after a long period of intellectual doubt the tortured seeker does at last attain to a clear faith, the discovery he commonly makes is not so much a *de novo* discovery of God as the discovery that he has really been believing in God all the time. What he sees, when the mists clear, is not some hitherto unsuspected reality; he sees rather that that which he has all along been believing in, and resting upon, and living by, that which has kept his love burning bright even while his faith burned dim, was nothing other and nothing less than God. And so he can only say, as Jacob said when morning broke over Bethel's stony fields, 'Surely the Lord is in this place, and I knew it not; ... This is none other but the house of God, and this is the gate of heaven.'[1] If we feel, as I think many of us do, that the relief of our own doubts came to us, not so much by the discovery of some reality which had hitherto been utterly unknown to us, as by a deeper insight into

[1] Genesis xxviii. 16 f.

the true nature of a reality which had been with us from the beginning, then we may be pardoned for believing that this reality is likewise within the experience of those of our fellows whose doubts have not yet been relieved. 'Suppose', writes Mr. R. G. Collingwood in his *Essay on Philosophical Method*, 'there were a kind of knowledge in which a distinction existed between knowing better and knowing worse, but none between knowing absolutely and not knowing at all. In pursuing this knowledge we should begin, not with utter ignorance of the subject-matter or any part of it, but with a dim and confused knowledge, or a knowledge definite enough in some parts but confused in others, and in others fading away to the verge of complete nescience. In advancing our knowledge of these things we should say, not "I have discovered something that I never knew before", but "I have cleared up my thoughts about this matter, and see that what I once thought about it was a confused mixture of truth and error." '[1]

Furthermore, we are bound to recognize that there is a kind of denial of God which is more serious, more destructive of our spiritual life, than is the intellectual denial of His existence, namely the practical denial of His claims. We can come much nearer to obliterating the recognition of God that exists in the bottom of our hearts by denying God in our *deeds* than we can by denying Him 'with the top of our minds'. 'But wilt thou know, O vain man, that faith without works is dead?'[2] He who believes in the existence of God but lives as if

[1] p. 96 f.   [2] James ii. 20.

God were not, has fallen much further from God than he who has difficulty in believing in God's existence yet lives in such a way as often to put believers to shame— like Dr. L. P. Jacks's shoemaker who 'spent his breath in proving that God did not exist, but spent his life in proving that He did'.[1] And it is of course a fact that this practical denial of God's reality consorts, more often than not, with the most unquestioned intellectual acceptance of it. Men may continue to believe in God 'with the top of their minds' while consistently denying Him in that part of their souls which governs all their deeds. 'The devils also believe, and tremble.'[2] Surely then it is those whose every desire and deed deny God that come nearest to deserving the unhappy name of atheist, and not those whose denial is an affair mainly of the intellect. We should ask ourselves whether some who profess belief in God are not much more genuinely atheistical than are many of our rationalist and communist friends who take to themselves that name. The real unbeliever is not he whose life witnesses to a belief that he thinks he does not possess, but rather he whose life proves that he does not really believe what he thinks he believes. We might quote:

> Perplext in faith, but pure in deeds,
> At last he beat his music out.
> There lives more faith in honest doubt,
> Believe me, than in half the creeds.[3]

But it is on certain other words that we should prefer

---

[1] *Mad Shepherds.* [2] James ii. 19.
[3] Tennyson, *In Memoriam*, xcvi.

to rely. 'Lord, when saw we thee an hungred, and fed thee? . . . And the King shall answer and say unto them, Verily I say unto you, Inasmuch as ye have done it unto one of the least of these my brethren, ye have done it unto me.'[1] This cannot mean that we are judged by our fruits rather than by our faith, it can mean only that we are *known* by our fruits, and that if the fruits are truly manifest, some germ of faith must then be there, however unrecognized.

But let us look now at the other side of the case. I have laid it down that men may know God in the bottom of their hearts while denying Him 'with the top of their minds'; let me now lay it down that they cannot thus know Him *well*. I have said that the intellectual denial of God's existence need not at once and utterly destroy the foundations of our spiritual life; let me now say that it threatens these foundations from the beginning and tends, as time goes on, to undermine them more and more seriously. Here again it would seem that the case is not without its analogues in other fields. The philosophical denial of the existence of the external world does not destroy our consciousness of that external world, but I believe that it would, in the long run, tend to interfere with it. A man who persists in cultivating the *opinion* that this apparently solid frame of things is but the shadow of a dream will not in the end have as vivid a *sense* of its reality as that with which he began. Again, the denial of the existence of other minds, such as is professed by the philosophical solipsist, is not likely utterly

[1] Matthew xxv. 37, 40.

to destroy that consciousness of their existence which he shares with the rest of us, but we can well imagine that in the long run it will do real damage to the social side of his nature. Solipsism is not really as dangerous an opinion as it looks; and yet it can by no means be regarded as harmless. Similarly, I should say that philosophic atheism, while not being quite as utterly destructive a thing as it looks, is nevertheless bound to lead to disastrous and tragic consequences. It will be noticed that I have not spoken of the three cases in exactly the same terms. They are sufficiently alike to illustrate my point, but I do not suppose them to be precise analogues. Philosophical atheism is, I am sure, much *more* damaging to religion than is philosophical solipsism to altruism; and that again is more damaging to altruism than it (or subjective idealism) is to sense-perception. The reason for this is evident, namely, that though an intellectual factor is present in sense-perception as well as in morality, and in morality as well as in religion, this factor nevertheless bulks more largely in morality than in sense-perception, but less in morality than in religion.

The serious inadequacy of a faith that is not conscious of itself will indeed scarcely be doubted. If the seed of faith be not allowed to develop into the life of prayer and praise and worship, its proper growth is being arrested at the very root. It is impossible that the spiritual life should ever flourish save in the generous atmosphere of an unabridged Christian profession and practice. There is a long spiritual discipline to be traversed before we can hope that the ultimate beauty should be revealed to us. The believer, we must repeat, finds in the most familiar experiences of life a meaning and a presence which the unbeliever does not find in them; and it is on this basis alone that he is able to proceed to further experiences which the unbeliever cannot have at all.[1]

'*Nur der wirklich glaubt, der auch weiss, dass er glaubt, der sich zu den Erwählten gehörig weiss*'—'Only he truly believes who also knows that he believes and knows himself to belong to the company of the elect.'[2] The words are Dr. Brunner's and, remembering the *wirklich*, we may perhaps take them as a recognition of the double truth on which we have been insisting; that a man may be in some way putting his trust in God without realizing that he is so doing, and may be held of God without knowing that he is so held; yet cannot, while this condition lasts, lead any but a very impoverished spiritual life. This teaching was familiar to the early Protestant theologians, who distinguished between *fides directa* and *fides reflexa* and maintained that the former might exist without the latter. A man, it was taught, may be a believer without certainly knowing that he is a believer. The certain knowledge that one is a believer is rather a final blessed fruit of belief than its necessary and inevitable accompaniment. 'Such as truly believe in the Lord Jesus', declares the Westminster Confession of Faith, '... may in this life be certainly assured that they are in

[1] *Supra*, p. 53. For a fuller discussion both of the reality of unconscious faith and of its inadequacy see D. M. Baillie, *Faith in God and its Christian Consummation* (1927), pp. 182–8.
[2] *Um die Erneuerung der Kirche* (1934), p. 17.

a state of grace. . . . This infallible assurance doth not so belong to the essence of faith, but that a true believer may wait long, and conflict with many difficulties, before he be a partaker of it; yet . . . he may, without extraordinary revelation, in the right use of ordinary means, attain thereunto.'[1] Such a statement, far from making too much of the knowledge that one is a believer, makes (as it seems to me) too little of it. It makes assurance too little necessary to the normal Christian life. And this, on the whole, has been the tendency of orthodox Protestantism, as distinct from Anabaptism and Methodism. 'The events spoken of and promised in the Word (that is to say regeneration)', wrote Franz Delitzsch in his text-book of biblical psychology published in 1855, 'take place in the depth of our consciousness, and only now and then do reflexes of them make their appearance in our consciousness. . . . The *actus directus* already has God's promise in itself. The *actus reflexi* . . . do not belong to the essence of justifying faith, the *actus directus* being, as our forefathers said, the *forma fidei essentialis*.'[2] But if such teaching goes too far in one respect, there is another respect in which it does not go far enough. It more than amply allows for the authenticity of a faith that is not conscious of itself, but it seems to allow this only, or mainly, with regard to one element in faith, namely the

[1] Ch. XVIII, §§ 1 and 3.

[2] *Biblische Theologie*, pp. 298, 306. These and other passages are quoted by Dietrich Bonhoeffer in his book *Akt und Sein* (1931), p. 155, where he himself adds: 'Das Hangen am Christus braucht sich seiner selbst nicht bewusst zu werden'—'Dependence on Christ does not need to be conscious of itself.'

element of personal trust and reliance. Three elements have been distinguished in faith by the theologians, *notitia*, *assensus*, and *fiducia*—information, assent, and trust. The Westminster Confession boldly asserts that there may be a faith in which the *fiducia* is not *reflexa* or conscious of itself; but does it allow the possibility of a faith in which the element of assent is not conscious of itself? The answer is that it does allow this with regard to children and imbeciles, but not with regard to those who have attained intellectual maturity. 'Elect infants, dying in infancy,' we read, 'are regenerated and saved by Christ through the Spirit, who worketh when, and where, and how he pleaseth. So also are all other elect persons, who are incapable of being outwardly called by the ministry of the word'; but 'men not professing the Christian religion' cannot 'be saved in any other way whatsoever, be they ever so diligent to frame their lives according to the light of nature, and the law of that religion they do profess; and to assert and maintain that they may, is very pernicious, and to be detested.'[1] The Church of Scotland, however, has wisely adopted two Declaratory Acts (of 1879 and 1892) in which it not only protects itself from the horrible suggestion that there are some dying in infancy whom God has not thus elected, but also extends the possibility of the exercise of God's grace to those not professing the Christian religion. It will suffice to quote from the earlier Act: 'That while none are saved except through the mediation of Christ, and by the grace of His Holy Spirit, who worketh when,

[1] Ch. X, §§ 3 and 4.

and where, and how it pleaseth Him; while the duty of sending the Gospel to the heathen, who are sunk in ignorance, sin, and misery, is clear and imperative; and while the outward and ordinary means of salvation for those capable of being called by the Word are the ordinances of the Gospel: in accepting the standards, it is not required to be held that any who die in infancy are lost, or that God may not extend His grace to any who are without the pale of ordinary means, as it may seem good in His sight.'[1]

If we ask why such a body as the Westminster Assembly found it more difficult to conceive of an assent that was not conscious of itself than of a trust that was not thus self-conscious, the answer is apparent. It is that the members of that Assembly were too intellectualistic in their interpretation of Christian faith, too much in love with credal orthodoxy, too ready to understand revelation as consisting in communicated information. But for us there is no reason why we should not extend the distinction between *fides directa* and *fides reflexa* to the element of *assensus* as well as to that of *fiducia*, and speak of an unconscious assent.

The truth is that an over-confident orthodoxy can be just as pharisaical as an over-confident righteousness, so that we must as much beware of regarding right belief as of regarding right conduct as a secure possession about which we may boast. If it was said, 'Not of works, lest

---

[1] *Declaratory Act of the United Presbyterian Synod* (1879), § 4. Cf. *Declaratory Act of the General Assembly of the Free Church of Scotland* (1892), § 3.

ny man should boast',[1] so it must also be said, 'Not of creed, lest some other man should boast of that'. We who know that we believe in God have received no right to deny that His saving power is at work also in the lives of those who do not know that they believe in Him—or in His Son Jesus Christ our Lord. An unself-conscious faith may also in its measure be a *fides salvifica*. With Professor Tillich we must be ready to allow that there is a 'justification of the doubter' no less than a justification of the sinner.[2] Yet it is clear that there *can* be no justification of the doubter if the faith that justifies and saves is always to be identified with a faith that is fully conscious of itself. For on no account must we, giving way to Pelagianism or semi-Pelagianism, allow that we can be justified by anything else than faith in God. 'To my mind', writes Professor Leonard Hodgson, 'the conscious faith in Christ which it is the privilege of the professing Christian to enjoy does not mark him off as more advantageously placed with regard to eternity than those who do not enjoy it; it enables him to recognize and interpret the unconscious faith of those whose eyes have not been opened to their true condition.'[3] 'What advantage, then,' he asks, 'has the Christian? Not the selfish joy of feeling superior to the rest of mankind, but the unselfish joy of giving his life in communion with His Master on behalf of all mankind who, equally with himself, are objects of God's love and will to save. There is

---

[1] Ephesians ii. 9.
[2] See P. Tillich, *Rechtfertigung und Zweifel.*
[3] *The Grace of God in Faith and Philosophy* (1936), p. 149.

perhaps no more striking evidence of the corruption wrought by sin in human nature than the fact that we find it so difficult to receive the divine revelation at this point.'[1] If only this revelation had been received, how many pages of ecclesiastical history would have made less ugly and depressing reading than actually they do!

[1] *The Grace of God in Faith and Philosophy* (1936), p. 97.

§ 8

In working out our conviction that all men believe in God, we have now come to see that they may nevertheless believe in Him in very different ways. In particular we have found ourselves distinguishing two ways of believing which fall short of the full Christian way. There is the man who has never doubted that God is, but who lives as though He were not; and there is the man who doubts whether God is, or even denies that He is, but lives as though He were. We have not hesitated to affirm that the former is much farther from the true Christian estate than the latter. And we have expressed our confident conviction that in the soul of the latter the saving grace of God is genuinely at work, though many of its most blessed fruits must necessarily be curtailed. The man who doubts or denies God with the top of his mind may nevertheless possess in himself, by the grace of the God whom he denies, the *forma fidei essentialis.*

But what now of the man to whom it has never occurred to doubt God's reality, but whose walk and conversation remain unaffected by his apparently unhesitating belief? What of the man about whom it was declared in one of the Declaratory Acts of the Church of Scotland referred to above 'that, in holding and teaching . . . the corruption of man's whole nature as fallen, this Church also maintains that there remain tokens of his greatness as created in the image of God; that he possesses a knowledge of God and of duty; . . .'?[1] Such a man believes and does not believe. He has one kind of faith in and knowledge of God, but lacks another. And the Christian Church has always taught that this lack is the most serious of all lacks that there can be in a man. For the kind of faith that this man lacks is the kind of faith that alone saves. The greatest and most important difference there can be between one man and another is that between him who possesses and him who does not possess this *fides salvifica*; though, as we have seen, he who does not possess it may have no conscious doubts of God's existence and he who does possess it may have such doubts.

Furthermore, the change that takes place in a man when he passes from the faith that saves not to the faith that saves is the most important of all changes that can take place in him. It is what we speak of as regeneration or conversion. We have often seen the change accomplish itself, and yet it is far from easy to offer a satisfying account of it. How, for instance, are we to describe the *awakening of conscience* which invariably accompanies it, and the *conviction of sin*? It is not as if the man did not previously *know* what things were sinful and what not sinful. It is not as if, up to this time, when he did that which was evil in the sight of the Lord, he did not know that he was doing evil. No, for (as was said in the passage just quoted from the Declaratory Act) he possessed from the beginning 'a knowledge of God and of duty'. In trying to describe the change we should say rather that

[1] Act of 1892, § 4.

though in a sense he was all the time aware of his sin, yet only now has it 'come home' to him. And so also with the saving faith in God and His Christ which goes together in conversion with the awakened conscience and conviction of sin. The new convert may long have known and believed all that the Church teaches about God and Christ, but somehow only now has the meaning of it all 'come home' to him. He has never, we say, 'taken it to himself' before. What is this 'coming home', this 'taking to oneself', which alone gives to faith a salvific power? It is, of course, something that God brings to pass in the soul; but perhaps it is more in the realm of the imagination that He brings it to pass than in the realm of the intellect. I have long been of opinion that the part played by the imagination in the soul's dealings with God, though it has always been understood by those skilled in the practice of the Christian cure of souls, has never been given proper place in Christian theology, which has too much been ruled by intellectualistic preconceptions. Yet it is not only in the sphere of religious belief that we are familiar with this difference between two ways of believing. I was told in my childhood that all men must die, and I had no thought of doubting the assertion, but it was long before I imaginatively took home to myself the meaning of this belief. And how often to this day do I read in the daily prints terrible statistics of the number of those killed and wounded in this or that war, or it may be in the traffic of our roads, or again of the number of the unemployed and homeless in the land, without imaginatively realizing the meaning of what I read! The late Bishop Gore once defined Christian charity as 'reading statistics with compassion'. It might be equally well defined as 'reading statistics with imagination'. For we are not naturally so cold-hearted that if the imagination were granted to us, the compassion would not follow.

But now the question may be pressed on us whether these two ways of believing—the belief in God which all men share and which the preacher assumes in his hearers, and the *saving* belief in God to which he summons them —are different kinds of belief or only different degrees of the same kind of belief. A careful answer to this question will, I think, reveal the fact that it is wrongly asked.

That saving faith does admit of many different degrees has indeed always been recognized. 'This faith', we read in the Westminster Confession, 'is different in degrees, weak or strong; may be often and many ways assailed and weakened, but gets the victory; growing up in many to the attainment of a full assurance. . . .'[1] The question we have now to raise, however, concerns the demarcation between the weakest degree of such saving faith and that belief in God which is general among men. Is that also but a matter of degree? Or is it marked by a clean line that has 'length but no thickness'? Since those who possess saving faith are said to be in a state of grace, and those who possess it not are said to be in a state of nature, this is the same as to ask, Is there a clean cut between the state of nature and the state of grace? Just, therefore, as

[1] Ch. XIV, § 3. The words seem to me to be borrowed from Calvin, *Institutio*, Bk. III, Ch. II, § 21 *ad fin.*

we concluded our first chapter by a consideration of the distinction between nature and revelation, so now we conclude the present chapter by a consideration of the distinction between nature and grace.

We have already spoken of conversion from the state of nature to the state of grace as being the fundamental fact of all religious experience. It would seem that all men everywhere realize this in some dim way. Those who are expert in the religion of savages have now for long been telling us that the fundamental conception of such religion is that of the supernatural power or influence known as *mana*. 'All Melanesian religion', wrote Bishop Codrington, 'consists, in fact, in getting this *mana* for oneself, or getting it used for one's benefit—all religion, that is, as far as religious practices go, prayers and sacrifices.'[1] It is clear that this conception plays in savage religion a part corresponding, in its crude and blind way, to the part played by the conception of grace in ours.[2] Moreover, in the savage's fundamental discrimination between the state of possessing *mana* and the state of not possessing it, it is impossible not to discern a crude groping after the distinction between grace and nature. There are, perhaps, few more backward peoples on the face of the earth than the Arunta tribe of Australian blackfellows described by Sir Baldwin Spencer and Mr. F. J. Gillen in their celebrated work on *The Native Tribes*

---

[1] *The Melanesians*, p. 125.

[2] This has been pointed out by Professor C. C. J. Webb, *Problems in the Relations of God and Man* (1911), pp. 89 ff.; by Professor N. P. Williams, *The Grace of God* (1930), p. 1; and by Martin Buber, *Ich und Du* (1923), p. 27.

of Central Australia; yet we cannot read the accounts there given of the four separate ceremonies of initiation which the young men are called upon to undergo —the tossing ceremony at the age of ten, the circumcision a few years later, the further operation of subincision a few months after that, and the fire-ceremony when full manhood is attained—without being convinced that even here there is present some dim and twisted recognition of the necessity of conversion and of the corresponding contrast between two states of being. Needless to say, as we pass from savage religion to the great ethnic cults, or to the mystery cults of the ancient classical world, this recognition becomes correspondingly more strongly marked.

To the question thus raised by the history of religion as a whole the Christian distinction between nature and grace is the only satisfying answer. It is true that the distinction does not appear in the New Testament in precisely these terms. St. Paul's distinction is rather between grace and *works*, i.e. between the undeserved favour of God in which he found salvation after his experience on the Damascus road and the keeping of the law in which he had previously failed to find salvation. But this state of works, as we may call it, may be taken as equivalent to what was afterwards spoken of as a state of nature. And St. Paul has other distinctions that are closely equivalent. One is that between the ψυχικός and the πνευμα-τικὸς ἄνθρωπος,[1] which the Vulgate translated as the *animalis* and the *spiritualis homo*, but which has usually

[1] 1 Corinthians ii. 14–15.

been rendered in English as the natural and the spiritual man. Closely connected with this contrast of ψυχή and πνεῦμα is the other contrast between σάρξ and πνεῦμα— flesh and spirit. St. Paul uses this contrast to explain his view of the convert as a new creation. 'Wherefore henceforth know we no man after the flesh. . . . Therefore if any man be in Christ, he is a new creation.'[1] And St. John, under the influence of St. Paul, uses it to explain his corresponding and characteristic view of conversion as a second birth or regeneration. 'That which is born of the flesh is flesh; and that which is born of the Spirit is spirit.'[2] Another pair of terms which is characteristically Johannine, though also Pauline, is that of life and death. Conversion (ἐπιστροφή) is regarded as a passing over (μετάβασις) from a state of death to a state of life. 'We know that we have passed from death unto life, because we love the brethren.'[3] 'He that heareth my word . . . is passed from death unto life.'[4] It is not until the year 200 and in the writings of Tertullian that we first find the contrast expressed in the terms which were to dominate later theological discussion. But there is no doubt that it was St. Augustine, 'the theologian of grace', who finally fixed their usage. One of his works, written early in 415, was entitled De natura et gratia, and was a reply to a treatise of Pelagius entitled De natura.

Now through all these variations of terminology we are aware of a single patient search for forms of expression which will adequately express the convert's sense

---

[1] 2 Corinthians v. 16–17. [2] John iii. 6.
[3] 1 John iii. 14. [4] John v. 24.

of contrast and cleavage between the old life and the new. No terms of contrast could seem more absolute than life and death, a new creation, being born again, and the word 'conversion' itself, which means 'a turning about' and suggests the picture of a man who has been heading in one direction and then turns directly about and heads in the opposite direction. This is well illustrated in the account of his conversion with which Tolstoy begins his little book called *What I Believe*: 'Five years ago I came to believe in Christ's teaching and my life suddenly changed; I ceased to desire what I had previously desired, and began to desire what I formerly did not want. What had previously seemed to me good seemed evil, and what had seemed evil seemed good. It happened to me as it happens to a man who goes out on some business and on the way suddenly decides that the business is unnecessary and returns home. All that was on his right hand is now on his left, and all that was on his left hand is now on his right.'[1]

It is clear that if we press these figures to the limit and insist, as it were, on squeezing the last drop of meaning out of them, we shall be making the severance between nature and grace an absolute one, and denying every sort of continuity between the two.

This is a view that has had considerable influence in the history of theological thought. We can well understand its motive, for it is a motive that we find working in ourselves. To magnify beyond all assignable limits the greatness of the change which God's grace has worked

[1] Aylmer Maude's translation.

in us may well seem a necessary part both of our confession of sin and of our thanksgiving. And yet it seems
certain that it is not the whole of Christian wisdom nor
the whole of the New Testament teaching. The theology
typical of the new convert is often not a very complete
theology, but is inclined to represent an outlook too
simple, too *simpliste*, to do justice to the delicate complexity of our total spiritual experience. The man whose
life has just been violently and suddenly revolutionized
by the grace of God may at once see very clearly the
most important thing of all, but there are also some
important things that he is more likely to realize later on,
rather than in this first access of joy and release. And
some converts there be who, just because they are too
ready to suppose that they have already learned all there
is to know, never come to see these later things at all.

Once, when my own thoughts on this matter were
most confused, I chanced to stand for a moment at an
Edinburgh bookstall, while waiting for a bus, and—
though with no intention of taking the *sortes virgilianae*—
lighted upon a passage which helped me greatly. It was
from an early and now long unobtainable volume by
my old teacher and revered friend, Principal Alexander
Martin; and here it is. 'Is there then no sort of connexion
between the natural life and the spiritual? Is there
nothing in the former leading on to the latter? nothing
to suggest it or to show that the need of it is felt even?
because if not, it will be said—if the severance is absolute
—it is difficult to see how any man will be able to pass
from the one to the other—even by the divine uplifting

—and remain the same creature still. The objection brings a great truth before us. The severance between the natural world and the spiritual is *not* just absolute after all. It is not exactly analogous to that, for example, between the kingdom of the living and the non-living. *For this natural man belonged to this spiritual kingdom once.* He is literally a degraded being, having fallen from his proper state into the many-wise evil plight in which we find him now. Therefore a great uneasiness possesses him. He can never quite rest in a world for which he was not created. . . .'[1] The title of the sermon in which the passage occurred was itself significant—'The Naturalness of the New Birth'. If we may speak of the naturalness of the state of grace, clearly the severance of grace from nature cannot be complete.

The debate over this issue has usually circled round the dictum of Aquinas that *gratia non tollit naturam sed perficit*—'grace does not destroy nature but fulfils it'. This, however, has sometimes led to confusion; for it is clear that much in our fallen natures, namely the sin in them, is in no sense fulfilled and perfected by grace, but only abolished and destroyed. Needless to say, nobody has ever understood this better than St. Thomas himself, and his dictum is in no wise intended as a denial of it. What he is anxious to affirm is only that the existing constitution of human nature contains in itself, and in spite of all the sinful corruption to which it has fallen victim, an implicit promise not merely of a state of grace to which it may one day be redeemed but also of a state

[1] *Winning the Soul, and Other Sermons* (1897), p. 242 f.

of glory to which it may finally be elevated. It is central to his whole apologetic that what is deepest in nature points forward both to grace and to glory.[1] This interest is, however, satisfied by any view which allows that, though there is much in nature with which grace must do away, there is also something which it conserves and fulfils. And to such a view we have already committed ourselves. In rejecting the doctrine of the total corruption of human nature we were really at the same time rejecting the doctrine of a complete discontinuity between nature and grace.

Nevertheless, this does not in itself solve our problem. St. Thomas does indeed recognize a continuity between nature and grace which such a Protestant document as the Westminster Confession refuses to allow, but he would agree with the Westminster Confession that this continuity has in itself no significance as regards salvation. The grace which is in nature is not a saving grace. If, then, by a state of grace we mean a state of saving grace, both authorities would agree in drawing a clean line between that state and the state of nature. That this has usually been regarded as the orthodox teaching there would seem to be no doubt. Any one man at any one moment is either in a state of grace or in a state of nature, either saved or not saved; there is no middle position; there is no middle class; it is a question not of degree but of kind.

It follows from this that the transition from the state

---

[1] Cf. the chapter entitled 'The Goal Postulated by Human Nature' in P. H. Wicksteed, *The Reactions between Dogma and Philosophy Illustrated from the Works of St. Thomas Aquinas*.

of nature to the state of grace always takes place in a single moment, a mathematical point of time. This is explicitly insisted on by many old theologians, both Roman and Protestant. According to the Catholic tradition the same man may oftentimes pass back and forth from the one state to the other. According to the prevailing Reformed tradition (confirmation of which, by his chaplain, Oliver Cromwell so eagerly sought with his dying breath) a man who has once passed into the state of grace can never fall away from it but will 'persevere unto the end'. On this latter view conversion can take place only once; and, though it may or may not be preceded by a long preparation, the conversion itself takes place at a mathematical point of time.

> Between the stirrup and the ground
> Mercy I sought, mercy I found.

There is, however, no question that such a view has its serious difficulties. The difficulty has been least felt by those Protestant sects, such as the Anabaptist, which have insisted on the necessity for every soul of a crisis of conversion after years of understanding have been reached, and have identified the transition from nature to grace with this crisis. But this is not a view that most of us are prepared to follow. We are not prepared to believe that our children who have been born and brought up in Christian homes in the nurture and admonition of the Lord are merely 'in a state of nature' until, having attained to years of greater understanding, they are 'confirmed in the faith'. That is why we baptize them in infancy. The Anabaptists, writes Calvin, 'infer that children are only to be regarded as sons of Adam until they have attained an age fit for the reception of the second birth. But all this is directly opposed to the truth of God. For if they are to be accounted sons of Adam, they are left in death, since in Adam we can do nothing but die. . . . But how, they ask, are infants regenerated, when not possessing a knowledge of either good or evil? We answer, that the work of God, though beyond the reach of our capacity, is not therefore null.'[1] Such also is the teaching of the Westminster Confession.[2] And in the pamphlet on Baptism prepared by the Church of Scotland Committee on Youth it is taught that in this sacrament 'the child receives God's gift of "new" life in Jesus Christ. He is engrafted into Christ—that is to say, he is made a member of Christ's Body, which is the Church. . . . *He is made a partaker of the benefits of the covenant of grace.* . . .'[3] Yet this must neither be taken to mean that the baptismal act itself infallibly assures salvation nor that the unbaptized are beyond the reach of saving grace. Says our Confession, 'Although it be a great sin to contemn or neglect this ordinance, yet grace and salvation are not so inseparably annexed to it, as that no person can be regenerated or saved without it, or that all that are baptized are undoubtedly regenerated.'[4] The Roman Church does indeed affirm that 'baptism is necessary to all for salvation', yet points also to a number of

[1] *Institutio*, Bk. IV, Ch. XVI, § 17. Beveridge's translation.
[2] Ch. XXVIII, § 1.
[3] *The Sacrament of Baptism*, p. 10.   [4] Ch. XXVIII, § 5.

things that may 'take the place of baptism' in cases where baptism is not available.[1]

Those who incline to the Anabaptist outlook are always apprehensive lest such teaching as the above should lead men to make light of the necessity of regeneration and conversion. The truth is, however, that regeneration is as vital to Paedobaptism as to Anabaptism, but that the conception of it is different. The Paedobaptist recognizes that children who have been brought up from earliest youth in the Church of Christ and in His nurture and admonition do not necessarily have to pass, at a later stage, through a single revolutionary crisis of conversion such as we associate with those who, like St. Paul and St. Augustine, were converted in adult life from other faiths. Confirmation in the faith is something quite different from conversion to the faith. Yet this does not mean that any can be saved without regeneration. In his famous Gifford Lectures William James contended that regeneration represented only one 'variety of religious experience', and that besides the 'twice-born type' there was also a 'once-born type' of saint whose experience, though essentially different, was equally authentic. This view has been accepted by many as a solution of our problem. Professor N. P. Williams in his admirable little book on *The Grace of God* makes a plea for the recognition of the rights of a 'once-born' type of theology side by side with the 'twice-born' theology of St. Augustine and his like. This, however,

[1] See, e.g., Cardinal Gasparri, *The Catholic Catechism*, English translation, Questions 162 and 360 of the 'Catechism for Adults'.

is an intolerably mistaken way of speaking. It is true that regeneration may accomplish itself in a variety of ways. It may do so in a single crisis, or again it may do so by imperceptibly gradual stages. It may be true, as was said by a master in the art of the cure of souls, that 'Lasting conversions are usually effected by degrees'.¹ It may be true, as Dr. Alexander Whyte was always quoting from one of his Puritans, that 'The perseverance of the saints is made up of ever new beginnings'. But in each and every case there must be a regeneration. There is no salvation for a fallen nature save in its re-making. 'Verily, verily, I say unto thee, Except a man be born again, he cannot see the kingdom of God.'²

It might now be supposed that a clean cut between the state of nature and the state of grace, though impossible to recognize in the case of those brought up from child-hood in the Church of Christ, would be easily recognizable in the case of those converted to Christianity from non-Christian religions. This, however, is very far from being the case. For not for a moment are we prepared to exclude utterly the adherents of other religions from the saving grace of God. The fact is, as we have already seen, that the distinction of grace from nature, far from being a distinction which merely divides Christians from non-Christians is a distinction which divides the experience of non-Christians themselves. Some kind of experience of conversion, in however warped and mistaken a form, is known *within* all the

¹ Père Nicolas Grou, *L'École de Jésus Christ*, xvi.
² John iii. 3.

religions, and not merely in the passage from these religions to Christianity.

Children of men! the unseen Power, whose eye
For ever doth accompany mankind,
Hath look'd on no religion scornfully
    That men did ever find.

Which has not taught weak wills how much they can?
Which has not fall'n on the dry heart like rain?
Which has not cried to sunk, self-weary man:
    Thou must be born again![1]

We need not subscribe to Matthew Arnold's whole conception of the mutual interrelation of Christianity and the other faiths in order to recognize the truth of these words. For how can we hold that the pagan or the Jew who has had a solemn experience of conversion within his own religious tradition is as little in a state of grace, and as completely in a state of nature, as he was before? Protestant theologians and confessions, as we have seen, have sometimes been inclined to be niggardly in their concessions on this point, but at least we were able to refer to the declaratory statement that in the Church of Scotland 'it is not required to be held that . . . God may not extend His grace to any who are without the pale of ordinary means, as it may seem good in His sight'.[2] The Roman Church has usually been more explicit. It teaches that 'God, who wishes all men to be saved, grants to all the graces they need for obtaining eternal life',[3] and that

---

[1] Matthew Arnold, *Progress.*   [2] *Vide supra*, p. 72.
[3] Gasparri, op. cit., 'Catechism for Adults', Q. 288.

accordingly God has made provision that he who is not baptized unto the Christian faith may be saved, 'if, through the operation of God's light and grace, he is— despite his invincible ignorance of the true religion— prepared to obey God and has been careful to keep the natural law'.[1] This is a matter on which we have of late been taught more wisely by none than by Baron von Hügel. Having strongly stated his conviction of the divinely appointed nature of the Christian and Catholic means of grace, he goes on to say, 'But this does not mean that noble, truly supernatural devotedness does not occur elsewhere in other Christian bodies, indeed also amongst Jews and Mohammedans, or amongst Parsees, Hindoos, and Buddhists, even amongst that apparently increasing mass of men who would be puzzled to say where they stand theologically at all'.[2] And in another essay he writes at greater length, 'But I believe the true scheme, as concerns religion, to have been best developed by Cardinal Juan de Lugo, the Spanish Jesuit, who wrote in Rome under the eyes of Pope Urban VIII, at the end of the seventeenth century. De Lugo first lays down that, according to Catholic doctrine, God gives light, suffi- cient for salvation, to every soul that attains to the use of reason in this life. He next asks, What is the ordinary method by which God offers and renders possible this salvation? And he answers that, though God doubtless can work moral miracles, these do not appear to be the rule, and are not in strictness necessary; that the human

[1] Ibid., Q. 162.
[2] *Essays and Addresses on the Philosophy of Religion*, 1st series, p. 281.

soul, in all times and places, has a certain natural affinity for, and need of, truth; and again, that the various philosophical schools and religious bodies throughout mankind all contain and hand down, amid various degrees of human error and distortion, *some* truth, some gleams and elements of divine truth. Now what happens as a rule is simply this: the soul that in good faith seeks God, His truth and love, concentrates its attention, under the influence of grace, upon these elements of truth, be they many or few, which are offered to it in the sacred books and religious schools and assemblies of the Church, Sect, or Philosophy in which it has been brought up. It feeds upon these elements, the others are simply passed by; and divine grace, under cover of these elements, feeds and saves this soul. I submit that this view admirably combines a sense of man's profound need of tradition, institution, training, with full justice to the importance of the dispositions and acts of the individual soul, and, above all, with a keen sense of the need of special graces offered by God to the several souls. And such a view in no way levels down or damps the missionary ardour. Buddhism does not become equal to Mohammedanism, nor Mohammedanism to Judaism, nor Platonism to Christianity, nor Socinianism, or even Lutheranism, to Catholicism. It merely claims that everywhere there is *some* truth; that this truth comes originally from God; and that this truth, great or little, is usually mediated to the soul, neither by a spiritual miracle nor by the sheer efforts of individuals, but by traditions, schools, and churches. We thus attain

an outlook, generous, rich, and elastic; yet also gradu-
ated, positive, unitary, and truly Catholic.'[1]

I cannot deny myself the pleasure of quoting still
another pronouncement on the matter from within the
Roman Church—from M. Jacques Maritain. 'The speculative refusal of God as a final end and as the supreme
rule of human life does not necessarily imply, for a mind
so blinded, a practical refusal to order one's life with regard to that same God, whose name is no longer known.
The Christian knows that God has infinite resource; and
that the possibilities of good faith stretch farther than
men imagine. Under many names, names which are not
that of God, in ways only known to God, the interior
act of a soul's thought can be directed towards a reality
which in fact truly may be God. For, as a result of our
spiritual weakness, there can easily be a discordance
between what in reality we believe and the ideas in
which we express to ourselves what we believe, and take
cognizance of our beliefs. To every soul, even to one
ignorant of the name of God, even one reared in atheism,
grace offers, at the moment when the soul deliberates
with itself and chooses its final end, grace offers as an
object, as something to be loved above all things, under
whatever name the soul describes such an end to itself—
but it is then a case (and this is the whole question to
which God alone knows the answer) of its thinking under
that name of *something other* than it signifies, of going
beyond the false name—offers that Reality of absolute
goodness, which merits all our love and is able to save

[1] Op. cit., p. 252 f.

93

our life. And if this grace is not rejected, the soul in question, in its choice of that reality, believes obscurely in the true God and really chooses Him, even when in good faith it is in error and adheres, not by its own fault, but by that of the education it has received, to a philosophical system of atheism, and conceptualizes this faith in the true God under formulas which deny Him. An atheist of good faith would thus, against his own apparent choice, really choose God as the true end of his life.'[1]

It would thus appear that no point can be found at which we can draw a clean line between grace and nature, and say that below this line the kingdom of grace does not extend *at all*. But now some orthodox theologians would reply, 'It is true that we cannot see the line, but God sees it. There is indeed no way by which we can tell who are in a state of nature and who in a state of grace, nevertheless some men *are* in the one state and some in the other, and there is no middle position. And God knows which men are in which state.' This may look like a humble acknowledgement that the judgement is of God and not of ourselves, but we should consider whether actually it may not be the very reverse. Actually we are judging when we so speak. We are affirming that some men are utterly outside the saving grace of God, though we are at the same time admitting that we do not at all know who these men are. That is a judgement, and it is not a particularly humble one. For the question now arises, If we cannot see a clean cut between the kingdom of nature and the kingdom of

[1] *True Humanism* (Eng. transl. of *L'Humanisme intégral*), p. 56 f.

grace, why should we suppose that it is there for God to see? It seems certain, as we began by noting, that the distinction we possess between nature and grace has come to us from the experience of regeneration, and that its dogmatic elaboration by the two great 'theologians of grace' was worked out by them on the basis of their own experiences of regeneration; but if a careful consideration (some lines of which we have attempted to indicate) of all that is implied in such regeneration does not itself yield to our observation a clean-cut division between some who are completely in a state of grace and others who are completely in a state of nature, why then should we believe that in reality the division is of this kind?

We have therefore to consider seriously whether we do right in supposing that the abrupt dichotomy between the two states, and the two classes of men, represents the divine point of view. May it not rather represent a point of view that is all too human? Is it not rather our blindness, our hastiness, and our lack of charity, that sees only black and white, when God sees many shades of grey? Certainly it would seem that it is not the crudest but rather the maturest human spirituality that finds the line most difficult to draw, and that discerns something of good where others find nothing but ill. There is indeed an opposite pitfall into which we are hardly less prone to fall, the pitfall of denying altogether the distinction between sinner and saint. We must here beware of shuffling with the accusations of our own conscience. Yet in avoiding this extreme we need not take refuge in the other. The highest human insight seems to point us to a difficult and delicately balanced position between these two easy ones. While taking full account of all there is in our Lord's discourse about the separation of the righteous from the wicked, the sheep from the goats, we cannot but remember how characteristic it was of Him to recognize the germ of saving faith in men and women who were as far as possible below the line which the Pharisees so confidently drew. If there were any whom He seemed to exclude utterly, it was those who were so sure that others were excluded.

Salvation means fellowship with God. The state of being saved is the state of being in fellowship with Him. To believe that some men are *wholly* out of such fellowship is the same as to believe that they are totally corrupt; for good in the creature can result only from fellowship with the Creator, who is the alone Source of all the good there is. But I have already argued that a creature from which the image of God was thus wholly effaced would not any longer be a man at all.

It was a great Christian poet who wrote:

To wisest moralists 'tis but given
To work rough border-law of Heaven,
Within this narrow life of ours,
These marches 'twixt delimitless Powers.
Is it, if Heaven the future showed,
Is it the all-severest mode
To see ourselves with the eyes of God?
God rather grant, at His assize,
He see us not with our own eyes!

Heaven, which man's generations draws,
Nor deviates into replicas,
Must of as deep diversity
In judgement as creation be.
There is no expeditious road
To pack and label men for God,
And save them by the barrel-load.[1]

It will thus be seen how cordially I agree with the Archbishop of York in the criticism he passes alike on the fourfold Medieval scheme of Heaven, Purgatory, Limbo, and Hell, and on the simplified Protestant dichotomy between Hell and Heaven. 'The scheme', he writes, 'presents certain administrative difficulties. It involves, in practice, the drawing of a sharp line between the awakened and the unawakened soul, and again between the pardonable and the unpardonable. But unless it be held—as in fact I find myself driven to hold—that these difficulties are insoluble in principle, it may be urged that they are soluble to omniscience, which, *ex hypothesi*, is available for the purpose. There are many of us, how-ever, to whom the difficulty mentioned is so overwhelm-ing as to make the whole scheme unreal, however watertight it may be dialectically. And I have not hesitated to speak of it in terms which indicate that sense of unreality. For the human soul is at once too delicately complex, and too closely unified, to be dealt with by any method of classification into mutually exclusive groups. ... The scheme is unworkable in practice even by omni-science, and moreover it offends against the deepest

[1] Francis Thompson, *A Judgment in Heaven*, Epilogue.

97

Christian sentiments. . . . There is a very strong case for thinking out the whole subject again in as complete independence as possible alike of medieval and of Protestant traditions. The reaction from the Middle Ages here as elsewhere has worked itself out.'[1] To this I would only add that in my view the scheme is *less* workable by omniscience than by our human short-sightedness; because, as our human understanding of the souls of men grows deeper and more Christian, the more difficult do we ourselves find it to justify the uncharitably hard lines of division which it is our natural tendency to draw.

It is natural that the doctrinal divergence of Dr. Brunner from Dr. Barth regarding the relations of nature and revelation should closely reproduce itself in regard to the relations of nature and grace, and it is natural also that our own attitude to the dispute should be the same in both cases. Just as formerly Dr. Barth would allow no general revelation, so now he will allow no general grace. Dr. Brunner, before proceeding to criticize his opponent's view, offers the following summary of it: 'It follows from the acknowledgement of Christ as the only saving grace of God that there exists no creative and sustaining grace which has been operative ever since the creation of the world and which manifests itself to us in God's maintenance of the world, since in that case we should have to recognize two or even three kinds of grace, and that would stand in contradiction with the singleness of the grace of Christ. . . . Similarly, the new

[1] W. Temple, *Nature, Man and God*, pp. 454-6.

creation is in no wise a fulfilment but exclusively a re-
placement accomplished by a complete annihilation of
what went before, a *substitution* of the new man for the
old. The proposition, *gratia non tollit naturam sed perficit*,
is not true in any sense but is·altogether an arch-heresy.'[1]
Such an opinion Dr. Brunner emphatically rejects, showing himself as anxious as we have been to find the grace
of God present within the state of nature, and as unwilling to believe that it is altogether withheld from any
human soul. But just as previously we found him holding that the general revelation granted to all men was a
completely different kind of revelation from the special
revelation granted only to Christian believers, so now
we find him holding that this *sustaining* grace is completely different in kind from the *saving* grace which is
in Christ alone. 'God', he writes, 'is near even to His
sinful creature who is far away from Him. It is precisely
this opposition of the divine nearness and the human
farness that is determinative. It finds expression in the
already-mentioned dual concept of nature. The manner
of God's being near to His fallen creature is his *sustaining grace*. Sustaining grace does not remove sin, but it
removes the extreme consequences of sin.'[2] That is to
say, it is God's sustaining grace that keeps unregenerate
men from being much more desperately vicious, and
society from being much more dissolute, than these
often are. To this Dr. Barth replies by asking what *grace*
there is in restricting men from vice and in keeping their

[1] *Natur und Gnade*, p. 8.   2/5845
[2] Ibid., p. 15.

society more or less decent and orderly, if it be not at all with a view to their salvation and if their ultimate end be only destruction and damnation. That, at least, is how I understand the somewhat difficult pages from which I can here quote only the following passage: 'How can we interpret the creation and its maintenance other-wise than in the light of the atonement? How can we speak of it otherwise than in the light of the revelation of Christ in the Old and New Testaments? And how can we carry over into the Bible the abstraction between creation and atonement? Does not all that Brunner calls a special "sustaining grace" appear there in relation with prophecy and fulfilment, with law and Gospel, with the covenant and the Messiah, with Israel and the Church, with the children of God and their coming salvation? Where has Brunner read there about another and abstract sustaining grace? But since he will have it so, we must further ask of him, How far is his sustaining grace then grace at all? Does this deserve to be called "grace"—that ever and again we are indeed allowed to live among conditions that shelter us from at least the grossest mis-demeanours and mishaps? Considered in itself, could not this quite equally well signify our condemnation to a sort of forecourt of Hell? If it signifies something different—and it truly does signify something different! —then it is certainly not merely for the sake of our being *sustained*!'[1]

Such a criticism against the half-way house which is Dr. Brunner's position seems to me quite final, indeed

[1] *Nein!*, p. 20 f.

devastatingly so. We gain nothing by admitting the operation of the grace of God in the wider sphere if we then go on to deny that this grace is in any least degree a saving grace. We gain nothing by admitting a continuity between nature and grace if in the next moment we deny all continuity between the grace that saves and the grace that only sustains. We have merely changed our terminology without widening our outlook or making it any more gracious—for, as Dr. Barth says, there is nothing gracious about a grace that sustains with no intent to save. Just as we said above with regard to the question of revelation, so we now say with regard to the question of grace, that we must travel much farther away from Dr. Barth's position than Dr. Brunner has done before we can find a halting-place which is capable of an equally valiant defence but about which it cannot be said, as the late Dr. H. R. Mackintosh has said about Kierkegaard's teaching under this head, that 'it is an attempt to teach God how large is the scope of His own severity and to improve on His ineffably gracious ways with men'.[1]

How then, finally, are we to answer the question from which we set out, as to whether the belief in God to which the preacher makes appeal as being in the bottom of all men's hearts and the saving belief in Him to which it is his office to summon them are two utterly different kinds of belief or represent but different degrees of one and the same belief? I believe the answer lies in realizing that the distinction between degree and kind on which

[1] *Types of Modern Theology*, p. 262.

this question relies is a distinction which was first devised as an aid to the scientific classification of physical objects, and which has proved itself to be an instrument admirably adapted to that end, but which cannot, without doing violence to the delicate facts, be applied without modification within the domain of things mental and spiritual. I should say that the two ways of believing do differ in kind, but that nevertheless there is a certain continuity between them. The difference between them, as we have seen, has often and rightly been expounded as the difference between a belief that is held theoretically without imaginative realization of its meaning and a belief that 'comes home' to a man in its bearing on his own case; yet it is clear that without some small degree of such realization of its meaning and bearing, a belief would not be a belief at all or in any sense, but only a meaningless and 'bearingless' form of words. There can be no belief in which the imagination as well as the intellect does not play *some* part. Yet in spite of this, the gulf between the unawakened and the awakened conscience may be so great as to be accountable psychologically for the greatest and most revolutionary upheaval in the whole range of human experience. It is thus possible to hold that the self-same image of God, which by the power of Christ is restored in the souls of the saints, is to be found dimly and brokenly reflected in all human nature, behind and below the ravaging defacements of sin's corruption; and at the same to magnify to the uttermost the implacably urgent need of the restoration itself, of the new creation and the new birth. In returning this answer

I have been greatly fortified by the study of a book from which I have already quoted once, Mr. Collingwood's *Essay on Philosophical Method*. The writer's main contention is that it is impossible rigidly to apply the traditional theory of scientific classification to what he calls philosophical concepts, by which he means the concepts used in the interpretation of our mental and spiritual life. Here is a sphere in which adjacent classes, instead of being mutually exclusive as they are both in mathematics and in natural science, always to some extent 'overlap'. This implies that 'the species of a philosophical genus do not differ merely in degree, nor merely in kind',[1] but in a way which combines the two. So Mr. Collingwood's doctrine of 'the overlap of classes' leads up to his doctrine of 'the scale of forms'. 'The combination of differences of degree with differences of kind', he writes, 'implies that a generic concept is specified in a somewhat peculiar way. The species into which it is divided are so related that each not only embodies the generic essence in a specific manner, but also embodies some variable attribute in a specific degree. In respect of the variable, each specific form of the concept differs from the rest in degree; in respect of the manner in which the generic essence is specified, each differs from the rest in kind. In such a system of specifications the two sets of differences are so connected that wherever the variable, increasing, or decreasing, reaches certain critical points in the scale, one specific form disappears and is replaced by another.'[2] It is clear, I think, that belief is a concept of

[1] p. vi. [2] p. 57.

this type. There is accordingly no good reason why zeal should lead to intolerance, or charity to lack of zeal.[1]

[1] Though I have made little reference to it in the text, I must not leave the subject without testifying to the great help I have received in the clarification of my thoughts concerning it from the writings of Professor Webb, especially from the two chapters on Nature and Grace in his *Problems in the Relations of God and Man*.

CHAPTER III

IS OUR KNOWLEDGE OF GOD'S EXISTENCE INFERENTIAL?

§ 9

IT has been the prevailing habit of Western philosophy to regard the existence of God as a conclusion, the truth of which is not known to us until we establish it by means of argument. The conclusions both of mathematics and of natural science are obviously of this kind, and it has been supposed that the existence of God is a conclusion of this kind too. There is indeed another and very different tradition which it is possible to trace through almost the whole history of the thought of the West, but undoubtedly the dominant tradition has been that just described. Nor are its origins at all mysterious to us. They are to be found in ancient Greece, and in that very episode in Greek intellectual history to which reference was made at the beginning of the last chapter. Until the age of the Sophists the existence of God or of the gods did not need to be defended in Greece, because nobody, so far as was known, had ever doubted it. But now it was not only being doubted but was being very dogmatically denied by many teachers of youth; and no small number of their pupils was following them in this denial. It was with this situation that Plato had to cope, and the way in which he met it was to set the standard for more than two thousand years of philosophical and theological thought. What he did was to meet the atheists on their own ground, not doubting the legitimacy of their approach to the question, but accepting their approach and, as it were, doing his best to beat them at their own game. They were claiming that the new science ruled God out; he would show that, on the contrary, it for the first time established His existence beyond all doubt. There is no way, said Plato, of reaching any certainty about God *except* through science—and, in particular, through the two special sciences of kinetics and astrophysics. 'No mortal man', he writes, 'can be secure in his religion (βεβαίως θεοσεβής) who does not possess these two things.'[1] Plato then was the first to think of proving God's existence by argument;[2] it is in his pages that the phrase 'proof of the existence of God' (ἀπόδειξις ὡς εἰσὶν θεοί)[3] is first found; and it is he who first represented the view that it is only by means of such proofs that we can ever reach full assurance of God's reality. From Plato this tradition passed into the Academy; through his pupil, Aristotle, it passed into the Lyceum; and finally it passed from both schools alike into the philosophy and theology of the Christian world. Moreover—though into this we need not go—it was not only the assumption of the necessity of such proofs that was thus taken over, but also the two particular proofs which Plato had constructed and which, with little essential variation, have remained orthodox down to our own time.

It will form a convenient basis for our future discussions if we now set out in some little detail the views concerning God's existence of the greatest and most

[1] *Laws*, Bk. XII, 967d.
[2] Unless, indeed, we are to ascribe the teaching of *Phaedo*, 97 ff., to the historic Socrates.
[3] *Laws*, Bk. X, 893b, &c.

influential of all the Christian philosophers of the Middle Ages, namely, St. Thomas Aquinas.

We have, according to St. Thomas, no *direct* knowledge of any existence save the world of nature as perceived by the five senses. Our knowledge of all non-sensible realities is discursive in character, being reached by inference from the things we can see and touch. God is of course a non-sensible reality, and hence He cannot be known to us directly or *per se*, but only *per suos effectus*, through His effects in the world of nature, *per ea quae facta sunt*, through the things which He has made.[1] 'The only road'—so his modern disciple, M. Étienne Gilson, sums up his teaching—'which can lead us to a knowledge of the Creator must be cut through the things of sense. The immediate access to the Cause being barred to us, it remains for us to divine it with the help of its effects.'[2]

St. Thomas then goes on to assess the extent of the knowledge of God which is thus obtainable by us. His conclusion is that we can have positive knowledge of His existence but only negative knowledge of His nature. We can know *that God is* and *what He is not*. Once we have established that He is real, it is only by this negative method, this *via negationis*, that we can proceed to determine what He is like. Thus, for example, we are able to prove that He is not plural, that He is not corporeal, that He is not in space, that He is not ignorant, and that

[1] Cf., e.g., *Summa Theologica*, I. 2, ii; *Summa contra Gentiles*, i. 12.
[2] *The Philosophy of St. Thomas Aquinas* (English translation of *Le Thomisme*), 2nd edition, 1929, p. 64.

He is not evil—nay also, that He is not even good, in the sense in which men may be good. But as to what He positively is—'the divine essence (*substantia*) so far exceeds in its immensity every form to which our intellect reaches that we are unable to apprehend it in such a way as to know *what it is*'.[1] This is why the names we use for the attributes of God are all privative words, formed by the aid of a negative prefix—like infinitude, impassibility, and unchangeableness. It would seem that we can do no more than set God in contrast to the world He has created and say that, whatever it is, *that* He is not. Fortunately, however, that cannot be quite the whole truth. For the world He has created is not just any world, but a very particular kind of world, and in creating it He must have been giving expression to His own nature. A cause always leaves the imprint of its own character upon its effects. The nature of God must therefore, to some extent, be revealed in the works of His hands, and above all in His greatest work of which we have any natural knowledge, namely in man. The angels, of course, represent a higher order of creation even than man, and if we either were ourselves angels or could have any direct knowledge of their natures, we should have a still better clue to the nature of God. But in our own human natures a certain clue is given us. God indeed infinitely surpasses all human attributes. He is not good or kind or intelligent in the sense in which we apply these words to men. No quality can be applied *univocally* both to man and to God. Yet these qualities, even as we know

---

[1] *Summa contra Gentiles*, i. 14.

them in man and as we are accordingly able to conceive them in our minds, do provide a certain *analogy* to something that is in God. God is more than good in the human sense, but certainly human goodness brings us nearer to Him than does human badness. Although, therefore, the word goodness, when applied to God as well as to man, must not be used univocally, but only equivocally, that is much better than not being able to use it at all. Thus the negative method is eked out by the method of analogy, the *via analogiae*. A single passage may be quoted to illustrate this teaching. 'Our natural knowledge', he writes, 'takes its beginning from sense. Hence our natural knowledge can reach as far as it can be led by the things of sense. But, starting from sensible things, our intellect cannot reach so far as to see the divine essence; because sensible things, which are created by God, are not equal to the power of God which is their Cause. Hence from the knowledge of sensible things the whole power of God cannot be known; from which it follows that His essence cannot be seen. But because they are His effects and dependent on Him as their Cause, we can be led from them so far as to know that God exists, and to know concerning Him those things which must necessarily appertain to Him in virtue of His being the first Cause of all things, exceeding all that He has caused.'[1]

Such then is the extent of our natural knowledge of God; and for our ability to attain to it St. Thomas, like all the medieval doctors, is fully conscious of our debt to Plato and Aristotle. But, of course, what characterizes

---

[1] *Summa Theologica*, I. 12, xii.

St. Thomas, in common with all the Christian philosophy of the Middle Ages, and in contradistinction alike from ancient Greek philosophy and from the prevailing tradition of modern philosophy since the Renaissance, is his belief that in addition to this natural way of knowledge there is also open to us a supernatural way, the way of faith in the Scriptural revelation. Let us then try to understand how far, and in what respect, the way of faith is really a different way.

It is plain that St. Thomas regards Scripture primarily as a body of communicated information, and faith as the acceptance of such information upon authority. He repeatedly compares faith to a schoolboy's acceptance, upon the word of his master whom he trusts, of facts (such as the sphericity of the earth) for which he himself does not yet know the evidence. Yet in such acceptance of authoritatively communicated information reason has more than one important part to play. In the first place, reason must convince itself that the authority is a good one—that the proffered revelation is authentic and really comes from God. In the second place, though reason should be prepared to accept on well-established authority much that goes *beyond* its own power to discover, it should never accept anything *contrary* to what it can itself discover; there can never be a good enough reason for believing in the reliability of an authority which asserts what is itself unreasonable.

It would now seem that on such a view faith is no less dependent on the discursive reason than is natural knowledge itself; the only difference being that in the one case reason establishes directly the truth of the conclusion, but in the other case only the credibility of certain witnesses to this truth. If the natural knowledge of God, in deducing His reality from His effects, seemed to be at one remove from Him, faith would thus seem—far from providing us with a more immediate access—to be at two removes. And there is no doubt that the reader of the *Summa contra Gentiles* is apt to carry away with him some such impression as this of St. Thomas's position. The author is there arguing with unbelievers. He submits that Scripture has been provided with an amply sufficient authentication in those exhibitions of miraculous powers and those miraculous fulfilments of prophecy which accompanied its original communication;[1] and he appears to claim that this authentication possesses in itself full logical cogency such as to compel belief in all reasonable minds. But when, in other works, he comes to discuss with his fellow Christians the nature of faith, it soon appears that this is not the whole of his teaching. Faith is not really a logical compulsion to believe at second hand what we are impotent to establish at first hand. Faith is not merely an affair of the intellect, but is also an affair of the will. It is, in fact, a virtue—one of the Seven Cardinal Virtues. And it is a supernatural virtue, attainable only by means of a direct infusion of divine grace. This means that, in addition to the external signs by which revelation is accompanied, there is also by the grace of God a direct persuasion of its truth in the heart of the believer; and here St. Thomas approaches very

[1] *Summa contra Gentiles*, i. 6.

near to the Reformation doctrine of the *testimonium internum spiritus sancti*. He rejects the view that the prophets and other Scriptural authors were merely the mouthpieces of truths of which they had no interior persuasion but which were guaranteed to them only by external signs accompanying their utterance; and he submits that this same interior persuasion is granted also to those who in later ages read what they wrote. He will not have it that we can of ourselves believe what of ourselves we could never have known. How this teaching consorts with his apparent insistence on the full logical cogency of the external authentication of revelation, it is by no means easy to discover. Perhaps he would have said of that authentication what Francis Bacon was afterwards to say about natural theology, that 'it sufficeth to convince atheism, but not to inform religion', and about natural ethic that 'it sufficeth to check vice, but not to inform duty.'[1]

St. Thomas regards it as a very great blessing that Holy Scripture, besides offering additional knowledge of God to those who have already attained to such knowledge as reason can give, includes those truths which can be reached by reason side by side with those which cannot; since it is at best a favoured few who are capable of

---

[1] *The Advancement of Learning*, Bk. II. For St. Thomas's teaching regarding the part played in faith by the will, and the internal evidence by which revelation is accompanied, see especially P. H. Wicksteed, *The Reactions between Dogma and Philosophy illustrated from the Works of St. Thomas Aquinas*, pp. 177–82, and the passages there transcribed and paraphrased from St. Thomas; A. L. Lilley, *Religion and Revelation*, pp. 42–6; D. M. Baillie, *Faith in God and its Christian Consummation*, pp. 65, 124 f.

the sustained effort of philosophical reasoning which is necessary to their establishment, so that the vast majority of mankind would otherwise be prevented from having any knowledge at all. Thus Dante, having read the *Summae*, could write at the beginning of the next century, in the famous twenty-fourth canto of the *Paradiso*:

> In one God I believe
> Sole and eternal, moving all the heaven,
> Himself unmoved, with love and with desire.
> For such belief not only have I proofs
> From physics and from metaphysics, but
> 'Tis also given me by the truth which flows
> Through Moses and the Prophets and the Psalms,
> Through the Evangel, and through you who wrote
> As God's inspired guardians of the truth.

At the same time, St. Thomas is very anxious to make the point that for those of us who *are* trained in philosophy and are accordingly able to reach God's existence by logical argument, such argument then becomes the *only* ground of our assurance of His reality. The existence of God may indeed be believed by the ignorant on the ground of information given in Scripture, and known by the learned on the ground of satisfactory evidence found in the facts of nature, but the same person cannot at the same time both know it and believe it, since the knowledge renders the faith unnecessary. A man who is unable to think out a problem for himself may accept the solution on the authority of another; but if and when he succeeds in discovering the solution for himself, the attitude of believing on authority disappears from his mind. So St. Thomas reaches the principle: *impossibile est quod de eodem sit fides et scientia.*[1]

Does this mean that rational knowledge of God is superior to faith in Him? That depends, our author explains, on what you mean by superior. There are two respects in which 'we have a more perfect knowledge (*perfectior cognitio*) of God by grace than by natural reason'; first, that by faith we know Him more fully (*plenius*); and second, that we know Him more certainly. Yet, as regards the first point, this fuller knowledge does not mean a more direct knowledge. It does not mean that we now know Him in His essence or *per se*. In faith we are still joined to Him as to One unknown (*quasi ignoto*) and know Him only as One wrapped up in veils (*velaminibus circumvelatus*). The knowledge of faith is still a knowledge of Him through His effects, and is a fuller knowledge only in the sense that 'many more of His effects, and those more excellent, are shown to us'. And as regards the second point, though faith as belief upon authority must in *this* case (when the authority in question is God's authority) be altogether superior to any rational conclusion as regards its degree of certitude, yet it still remains inferior to it as regards the quality of its knowledge; since it is better to see a truth for oneself than to believe it on even the *best* authority. Faith then has the *maior certitudo*, but reason the *maior evidentia*. 'So far as vision is lacking to it, faith falls short of the order of

[1] *Qu. disp. de Veritate*; see E. Gilson, *The Philosophy of St. Thomas Aquinas*, pp. 41–4.

knowledge which is present in science (*deficit a ratione cognitionis, quae est in scientia*).' In such a statement no room seems to be left for the view of faith as a direct interior persuasion of the truth revealed, yet this is the kind of statement that St. Thomas always offers us.[1] And a like view has recently been defended by M. Gilson in his Gifford Lectures on *The Spirit of Mediaeval Philosophy.* 'There is', he writes, 'no question of maintaining—no one has ever maintained—that faith is a kind of cognition superior to rational cognition. It is quite clear, on the contrary, that belief is a *succedaneum* of knowledge, and that to substitute science for belief, wherever possible, is always a positive gain for the understanding. For Christian thinkers the traditional hierarchy of the modes of cognition is always faith, understanding, and vision of God face to face.' 'Like St. Augustine and St. Anselm before him, St. Thomas situates the reason of the Christian philosopher in an intermediate position between the faith which guides his first footsteps, and the full knowledge which the beatific vision will bring hereafter.'[2]

Such then is the knowledge of God which is possible to us. But what now of the third kind of knowledge which is mentioned more than once in these extracts, and which is acknowledged to be the highest knowledge of all—that direct knowledge of God, not as He is reflected in the world He created, but as He is in Himself, which is spoken of as *vision*? St. Thomas's teaching is quite clear. He knows well that this kind of knowledge is

---

[1] e.g. *Summa Theologica*, I. 12, xi–xiii.
[2] *The Spirit of Mediaeval Philosophy*, English version, p. 35.

altogether better than any other. His whole life is a yearning for it. His whole philosophy is an ascent towards it. He knows that it constitutes the only true beatitude. He believes with all his heart and mind that it will be granted to the beatified saints in heaven, when at last they are *in patria*. But he is no less firmly convinced that it is a mode of knowledge impossible to ourselves on earth, who are still *in via*. Vision, he writes, must always be lacking unless a man be separated from this mortal life (*nisi ab hac vita mortali separetur*).[1] The Bible does indeed tell us that Moses and Aaron, Nadab and Abihu, and seventy of the elders of Israel went up into the mountain and 'saw the God of Israel'.[2] This text (together with certain other apparent instances of vision in the Old Testament) presents a certain difficulty for St. Thomas's view, and he is always recurring to it. But he holds that such cases of vision being granted to *viatores* are not only exceptional, but essentially miraculous in nature; while at the same time being prepared to allow, if somewhat reluctantly, that similar miraculous visions have been granted to some of the greatest mystics.[3]

[1] *Summa Theologica*, I. 12, xiii.
[2] Exodus xxiv. 10.
[3] For the above account of St. Thomas's views I have depended mainly on the opening chapters of the two *Summae* and have consulted only a few of the *Opuscula*. But I have been greatly helped by Wicksteed's truly admirable volume, already referred to; also by R. L. Patterson, *The Conception of God in the Philosophy of Aquinas*, 1933; E. Gilson, *The Philosophy of St. Thomas Aquinas*; and the work already referred to by A. L. Lilley.

I have said that Plato's Greece was the source of the tradition according to which the existence of God requires and admits of proof by argument. Was, then, such a tradition wholly absent from the Palestinian and Scriptural background of Christianity? Let us see.

First, as to the Old Testament. Dr. Henry Sloane Coffin once preached a sermon in New York on the commandment 'Thou shalt have no other gods', which began with the words, 'Had this commandment been written for our day and place, it would rather have read, "Thou shalt have at least one God".' That puts very well the difference between Bible times and our own. The danger then was not that men should believe in no gods but that they should believe in too many. None of the Old Testament writers treats of the existence of deity as if it were an open question or in any sense problematic. They betray no consciousness that there were any in Israel who denied it. There are, indeed, three or four passages in the literature which look at first sight like exceptions to this statement, but a close examination of them shows that they are not so in reality. In the tenth psalm we read of murderous criminals who despise Jehovah and whose thoughts amount to the declaration that 'There is no God'. It is perhaps not entirely clear whether the poet has in mind inimical surrounding nations or certain Israelite freebooters who have been causing trouble, but in either case most of the commentators are concerned to make the point that this is 'not a denial of the divine existence, but of His presence and interposition'.[1] This is made clear enough by the rest of the psalm, where the thoughts in the criminals' minds are said rather to be 'God does not punish', 'God has forgotten, He has hidden His face, He never sees'. Again in the fourteenth psalm, which is the same as the fifty-third, we read of fools or impious men who say in their heart 'There is no God', but again the commentators make the point that it is God's effective presence rather than His existence that is being denied, so that we should perhaps translate 'No God is here'. Much the same may be said of the attitude of mind ascribed by Jeremiah to many of the inhabitants of Jerusalem, both the poor and ignorant folk and also those of high degree. Some translators render, 'They have denied Jehovah and said, He is not'; but others prefer to render, 'They have belied Jehovah and said, He will do nothing.'[2] It seems clear that in all these passages we have to do not with intellectual perplexity but with sinful evasion—with the wicked man's attempt to persuade himself that he can go through with his wickedness and yet escape divine judgement. As for the nations surrounding Israel, they had, of course, their own gods and did not worship Jehovah or trust either in His power or in His goodwill, but that such a deity as Jehovah existed it probably never occurred to them to question; just as the Israelites themselves never perhaps came to think the gods of the surrounding

[1] C. A. Briggs, *A Critical and Exegetical Commentary on the Book of Psalms*, vol. i, p. 77.   [2] Jeremiah v. 12.

nations out of all existence, though they did come to regard them as mere demonic 'powers of darkness' inhabiting the underworld. The question in those days was not 'What gods exist?' but 'What gods must I worship?'

It is therefore natural enough that no attempt should be made in the Old Testament to establish the divine existence by means of argument. In that same chapter of Jeremiah we do indeed find such a passage as the following: 'Hear now this, O foolish people, and without understanding; which have eyes, and see not; which have ears, and hear not; Fear ye not me? saith the Lord: will ye not tremble at my presence, which have placed the sand for the bound of the sea by a perpetual decree, that it cannot pass it; and though the waves thereof toss themselves, yet can they not prevail; though they roar, yet can they not pass over it? But this people hath a revolting and a rebellious heart; they are revolted and gone.'[1] This, however, is not an argument for God's existence but a reminder of the inexorable character of His commandments. And so it is generally. 'When psalmist or prophet', writes Sir George Adam Smith, 'calls Israel to lift their eyes to the hills, or to behold how the heavens declare the glory of God, or to listen to that unbroken tradition which day passes to day and night to night, of the knowledge of the Creator, it is not proofs to doubting minds which he offers: it is spiritual nourishment to hungry souls. These are not arguments—they are sacraments.'[2] It is not until we reach Philo that

---

[1] Jeremiah v. 21-3.   [2] *The Book of Isaiah*, vol. ii, p. 90.

we first find a Jew who acknowledges the existence of atheism and seeks to rebut it with argument; but it is Greek atheism that the Alexandrian has in mind and it is with the cosmology of Plato's *Timaeus* that he rebuts it! All through the Old Testament it is assumed that the knowledge of God rests, not on cosmological speculation, but on the revelation of Himself which He has vouchsafed—on the theophanies of Mount Sinai, on the laws He gave to Moses, on the words He spoke to the prophets.

In this respect, then, the Old Testament literature occupies the same position as that of Greek literature before the rise of the philosophic movement. Yet it is remarkable how often this fact was obscured from the minds of Christian scholars during the long reign of rationalism. It was hardly a welcome discovery to the early seventeenth century when Pascal wrote, '*C'est une chose admirable que jamais auteur canonique ne s'est servi de la nature pour prouver Dieu.*'[1] Nor was it even a very welcome discovery when 'Rabbi' Davidson set the facts on which we have been dwelling at the very forefront of his *Theology of the Old Testament*, published posthumously in 1904. 'On the subject of *God*', he wrote, 'the ideas of the ancient world are in many respects different from our own. And the ideas of the Old Testament have, in these points of difference, naturally greater affinity with those of the ancient world in general than with ours. One such point of difference is this, that it never occurred to any prophet or writer of the Old Testament to prove the

[1] *Pensées*, ed. Brunschvicg, iv. 243.

existence of God. To do so might well have appeared an absurdity. . . . Scripture regards men as carrying with them, as part of their very thought, the conception of God. . . . This being the case, the Old Testament naturally has no occasion to speculate on how this knowledge that God *is* arises in the mind. Its position is far in front of this. It teaches how God who is, is known, and is known to be what He is. But it seems nowhere to contemplate men as ignorant of the existence of God, and therefore it nowhere depicts the rise or dawn of the idea of God's existence on men's minds. . . . The Old Testament as little thinks of arguing or proving that God may be known as it thinks of arguing that He exists. Its position here again is far in front of such an argument. How should men think of arguing that God could be known, when they were persuaded they knew Him, when they knew they were in fellowship with Him, when their consciousness and whole mind were filled and aglow with the thought of Him, and when through His Spirit He moved them and enlightened them, and guided their whole history?'[1]

What we have said about the Old Testament applies to the New with but little variation. It is true that the concept of faith (πίστις) now comes to have an altogether greater prominence and that the root of all evil is seen to lie precisely in unbelief. According to the teaching of our Lord what is wrong with the world is precisely that it *does not believe in God.* Yet it is clear that the unbelief which He so bitterly deplored was not an intellectual

[1] pp. 30, 31, 34.

persuasion of God's non-existence but rather something that was wont to consort with the most undoubting intellectual persuasion of His reality. Those whom He rebuked for their lack of faith were not men who denied God with the top of their minds, but men who, while apparently incapable of doubting Him with the top of their minds, *lived* as though He did not exist. So far as our records show, He never had to deal with the kind of men to whom He would have to say, 'You think you do not believe in God, yet in the bottom of your hearts you know that you are surrounded by His holiness and love.' Rather had He to deal with men to whom He had to say, 'You think you *do* believe in God, yet you refuse to trust Him in every hour and circumstance of need.' Argument for God's existence was not at all what was needed in such a case, and it is not surprising that He did not offer any. When He bade men consider the flowers of the field, He was not—as has sometimes been supposed—using the argument from design to establish God's existence; He was using the argument *a fortiori* to make men put more trust in God's love.

What is true of the Gospels is true of the Epistles. Here again it is consistently taught that what is wrong with the world is its lack of faith or belief; yet again the belief that is lacking is of a kind that is quite compatible with the most unquestioned acceptance of God's existence. It is, of course, quite clear to us that saving faith in God the Father and in Jesus Christ His Son must include belief in God's existence as a necessary part and implication of it; but it is only rarely that the New Testament finds occasion to make this implication fully explicit. The most important passage is in the great chapter on faith in the Epistle to the Hebrews: 'For he that cometh to God must believe that he is, and that he is a rewarder of them that diligently seek him.'[1] I remember hearing one of the most distinguished of living Biblical scholars remark that those two little words, ὅτι ἔστιν—'that he is', always struck him as less Hebrew in their emphasis, and more Greek, than almost anything else in the New Testament. And Dr. Moffatt comments on them that they 'would appeal specially to those of the readers who had been born outside Judaism'.[2] There is also the passage already quoted from the Epistle of James: 'Thou believest that there is one God, thou doest well: the devils also believe and tremble. But wilt thou know, O vain man, that faith without works is dead?'[3] Though the reference is here not merely to the existence of God but also (in the true Hebrew fashion) to His unity, yet His existence does seem to be referred to explicitly. But such purely intellectual acceptance, though it must enter as a component part into a truly living faith, is held to be of little or no value in itself. There is plainly a touch of sarcasm in the words 'Thou doest well: the devils also believe and tremble.' The writer regards the intellectual recognition of God's existence as something that can be taken for granted in all men, and even in devils. Similarly, when St. Paul reminds the Gentile Ephesians that before their

---

[1] Hebrews xi. 6.
[2] *A Critical and Exegetical Commentary on the Epistle to the Hebrews*, p. 167.
[3] James ii. 19–20.

conversion to Christianity they were ἄθεοι, 'without God', he cannot be taken to mean that they did not in those days believe in the existence of any kind of God.[1] Finally, there is the other statement of St. Paul, which was before us in our first chapter, to the effect that 'ever since the creation of the world his unseen attributes, his eternal power and divinity, have been plainly seen in the things he has made'.[2] St. Thomas Aquinas took this to be the argument from design, but such a reading of it is undoubtedly mistaken. What is said is not that the works of God's hands prove His existence but that they reveal certain aspects of His nature; and this, once again, is carefully pointed out by most modern commentators.

Thus for the New Testament, as for the Old, God is One who is directly known in His approach to the human soul. He is not an inference but a Presence. He is a Presence at once urgent and gracious. By all whom He seeks He is known as a Claimant; by all whom He finds, and who in Christ find Him, He is known as a Giver. The knowledge of God of which the New Testament speaks is a knowledge for which the best argument were but a sorry substitute and to which it were but a superfluous addition. 'He that hath seen me hath seen the Father; and how sayest thou then, Shew us the Father?'[3]

Non in dialectica, said St. Ambrose, *complacuit deo salvum facere populum suum.*

---

[1] Ephesians ii.'12. 'In Greek, however, it does not have the meaning of denying the existence of God. . . . The word must in this place be taken to mean "ignorant of God's true nature".'—E. F. Scott, *The Epistles of Paul to the Colossians, to Philemon and to the Ephesians* (The Moffatt Commentary), p. 169 f.   [2] Romans i. 20.   [3] John xiv. 9.

§ 11

It would thus appear that the thought of our own time, in breaking (as it is undoubtedly doing over so wide a front) with the long dominance of the Greek tradition of theistic argumentation, is returning in a very significant way to the Biblical point of view. St. Thomas thought he could harmonize the two traditions by simply placing them side by side—a process which may be described as synthesis by juxtaposition. The Greek tradition, as we saw, gave him his *natural* knowledge, and the Biblical tradition his *revealed* knowledge. The former provided the first chapters in theology, and the latter the more advanced. That this has been the orthodox position not only in the Roman but also in the Reformed Church may be seen by consulting any such irreproachably orthodox handbook as Hodge's *Outlines of Theology*, where the first chapter argues in the Greek manner for God's existence, while from this point onwards reliance is placed almost exclusively on Biblical revelation. The present dissatisfaction with this facile distinction between a natural and a revealed knowledge of God rests ultimately on the perception that the Greek and Biblical approaches, instead of being in this way merely complementary the one to the other, represent rather fundamentally diverse modes of thought between which it is necessary, in the last resort, to make a choice.

It may be remarked in passing that exactly the same applies to the medieval attempt to harmonize the two ethical traditions. The Greek moral teaching recognized four cardinal virtues—wisdom, courage, temperance, and justice; and here also it was Plato who was the originator. The Biblical tradition recognized three cardinal graces—faith, hope, and charity. The solution of the scholastics again consisted in synthesis by juxtaposition; to the four Platonic virtues they added the Pauline three, so forming their list of the Seven Cardinal Virtues which they set in contrast with the Seven Deadly Sins. The first four they called the 'natural' virtues, and these provided the first chapters of their ethics; while the remaining three they called the 'supernatural' or 'theological' virtues, and these provided the more advanced chapters. Yet to us such a solution appears as mechanical, and as lacking in true historical understanding, as the corresponding distinction between natural and revealed theology. The Platonic and Pauline lists are, fundamentally, not complementary but rival statements, each claiming to cover in itself the whole necessary ground; so that, instead of attempting to accept them both as they stand, we must either work them into one another or else choose between them.

It was not until the second half of the eighteenth century that the traditional argumentation for the existence of God began to be seriously challenged; but, as is well known, it was then to come under the sweeping criticism of the two greatest thinkers of the period, namely, Hume and Kant. But it is necessary to distinguish three different forms which this criticism has assumed. First, it has been contended that the particular proofs on which natural theology had relied all turn out, on closer examination, to be invalid. Many would say, indeed, that the invalidity of these proofs has long ago been demonstrated *ad nauseam*, so that they are weary of the whole debate. One of our most eminent theologians recently said to me that he had some time previously made a vow with himself never to read another page on the theistic proofs.

Secondly, however, there has been a criticism which has directed itself not so much against the particular proofs as against the general idea underlying most of them—the idea, namely, that we can logically proceed from nature to God or, in the words in which we found M. Gilson summing up St. Thomas's teaching, that 'the only road which can lead us to a knowledge of the Creator must be cut through the things of sense'. Thus Kant follows up his famous criticism of the individual theistic arguments in *The Critique of Pure Reason* by a further section which carries us much more deeply into the heart of his thought, and which bears the title 'Critique of All Theology Based upon the Speculative Principles of Reason'. This does not mean, however, that Kant is averse to all argument directed to prove the existence of God. It is only 'speculative' arguments that he objects to—arguments based on what he calls the principle of reason in its theoretical exercise; which means nearly, though not quite, the same as St. Thomas's 'arguments drawn from things of sense'. He himself, as is well known, has an argument of another kind to put forward—an argument drawn not from the things of sense but from the things of conscience, an argument which reaches God not through the world of nature but through the realities of the moral life.

But there is a third and still more radical type of objection which has been taken to the traditional argumentation for the divine existence, and it is this third type of objection which has been determinative for the greater part of recent theological thought. If we turn from the pages of Kant's *Critiques* to the pages of a Schleiermacher, a Ritschl, a Herrmann, a Sabatier, a Karl Barth, or a Karl Heim, we find that the objection is no longer merely to the employment of arguments drawn from the facts of nature but to the employment of any arguments at all. It is true that a partial reservation must here be made with reference to Ritschl. It appears from the many hesitations and waverings of the constantly re-written introduction to the third and most important volume of his *magnum opus* that he was never quite able to make up his mind whether he should or should not accept Kant's moral proof as germane to his own thought. If Kant's proof is no more than is intended by the saying, 'If any man will to do his will, he shall know of the doctrine',[1] then he is entirely ready to accept it.[2] Yet he is clearly inclined to be impatient with this whole business of proof, and I think all students of Ritschl will be likely to agree that the attempt to prove God's existence by any sort of logical process is fundamentally foreign to his theological approach. It is, moreover, an interest-

[1] John vii. 17.
[2] *Justification and Reconciliation*, vol. iii, English translation from the 3rd edition, p. 226.

ing fact that in the fragmentary work which was found on Kant's desk after his death and an exhaustive digest of which was published by Dr. Adickes in 1920 under the title of *Kants Opus Postumum*, Kant himself is found veering round towards the view that God, instead of being merely reached by deduction from the profound experiences of the moral life, is Himself directly present to us in these experiences.[1] Professor Webb illustrates the view which was thus finally reached by Kant by means of a sentence from James Martineau: 'In the act of conscience we are immediately introduced to the Higher than ourselves that gives us what we feel.'[2] Beside that sentence I should like to place another from Professor H. H. Farmer's little book bearing the significant title *Experience of God*: 'Unless the conviction of God is given in and through the moral life, it cannot be reached by logical inference from the fact of the moral life.'[3] In an earlier writing of my own I was concerned to make the same point when I wrote: 'In the experience of moral obligation there is contained and given the knowledge, not only of a Beyond, but of a Beyond that is in some sort actively striving to make itself known to us and to claim us for its own.' 'For it is not merely that through our values we reach God or that from

[1] See *Kant Selections*, edited by Theodore M. Greene (New York, 1929), pp. 370–4; N. Kemp Smith, *A Commentary to Kant's Critique of Pure Reason*, 2nd edition, pp. 638–41; C. C. J. Webb, *Kant's Philosophy of Religion*, pp. 178–201.

[2] *Kant's Philosophy of Religion*, p. 193, quoted from Martineau, *A Study of Religion*, vol. ii, p. 27.

[3] p. 76.

them we infer Him, but rather that in them we find Him.'[1]

It is evident, then, that our real quarrel with the traditional argumentation for God's existence is of a very deep-going kind. We are rejecting logical argument of any kind as the first chapter of our theology or as representing the process by which God comes to be known. We are holding that our knowledge of God rests rather on the revelation of His personal Presence as Father, Son, and Holy Spirit. We are thus directly challenging St. Thomas's doctrine that we have no knowledge of God *per se* but only *per ea quae facta sunt*—through His effects in the world of nature, and are allying ourselves rather with that other strain in medieval thought, which was opposed by St. Thomas and about which more will have to be said in the next chapter—the doctrine represented by St. Bonaventure's dictum that God is present to the soul itself (*Deus praesens est ipsi animae*). Of such a Presence it must be true that to those who have never been confronted with it argument is useless, while to those who have it is superfluous.

Students of the history of philosophy have often confessed to the feeling that the massive and often passionate assurance of God's reality which has been professed by a majority of its leading figures did not really rest upon the arguments which they so painstakingly contrived for the establishment of His existence, these arguments being rather in the nature of afterthoughts, subsequent to their belief in Him rather than the cause of it, and therefore,

[1] *The Interpretation of Religion*, pp. 462, 470.

in the language of the new psychology, not so much reasons as rationalizations. It is, for example, difficult to believe that it was really in the procession of the fixed stars and in the analysis of the ten kinds of motion that Plato discovered God, though he speaks as if it were only there that any man could surely find Him. Nor again can we believe that it was in his 'new theory of vision' that Berkeley found Him, or Paley in the anatomy of the human eye, or Spinoza in his *philosophia more geometrico demonstrata*. These great men were not ignorant of God before they lighted upon these proofs of Him, nor would they, if these proofs had failed them, have kept their minds quite open to His non-existence until they had lighted on other and better ones.[1]

[1] 'Now if these thinkers engage in a mere speculative argument, it is with little profit either to themselves or others, because they are not really talking of the conception of God as it is for themselves; of the living reality of it in their own minds. In its true reality it cannot be seriously considered as a matter of argument. What they ought to do is to try to come to as clear a consciousness as possible of the nature of their conviction: that is the important thing and vital to science and philosophy; this is what they ought to do if they would help in a discussion like this. . . . Now some of those who seriously engage in argument are in this case; they are not aware of their true position and that it is their conviction which produces the argument and not the argument their conviction. . . . One sees this sometimes in the greatest philosophers. The arguments by which they seek to recommend some of their most important principles to others are clearly not the process by which they arrived at them themselves, for they are sometimes not only unsatisfactory but fallacious, and if they had not been so convinced of the truth of their conclusion, they would have seen that themselves. . . . One's first thought when trying to prove anything about God or morality should be—did I really get this conviction myself in this way? Then and then alone do we find the meaning and value of our own thoughts.'—J. Cook Wilson, *Statement and Inference*, vol. ii, pp. 849–51.

§ 12

THOUGH this is clear to the observer, it is remarkable how often it seems to have been hidden from the thinkers themselves. These have so often spoken as though the existence of God were a 'surprise' conclusion that greeted them at the end of their reasoning rather than a fact the recognition of which prompted the beginning of it. Yet not all have spoken thus. In the eleventh century St. Anselm, in embarking upon one of the most masterly and original treatments of the subject ever undertaken, makes it quite clear that in his view the office of argument is not to give rise to belief but only to enable us to understand what we believe already. His *Monologion* he describes as an *exemplum meditandi de ratione fidei*, that is, an object-lesson in reflection upon the logical structure of the belief we already possess; while his shorter and more famous *Proslogion* is described as *fides quaerens intellectum*, 'belief in search of understanding'.[1] Not only does the belief precede the argument but it *must* so precede it; for the argument seeks to understand the belief, and if we have no prior belief, there is nothing there for us to understand. 'I make no attempt to penetrate Thy sublimity, for in no wise do I measure my understanding against that; but I long in some degree to understand that truth of Thine, which my heart believes and loves. For I do not seek to understand in order that I may believe, but I believe in order that I may understand.

[1] *Proslogion*, Preface.

For this also I believe—that unless I believed, I should not understand.'[1]

It has sometimes been supposed that in enunciating this celebrated principle, *Credo ut intelligam*, 'I believe in order that I may understand', St. Anselm meant only that we begin, and rightly begin, by believing upon *authority* what we afterwards go on to *justify* rationally, thus substituting personal conviction for our former blind acceptance of tradition. Such an interpretation, however, does much less than justice to the profundity of the great Archbishop's thought. It presupposes a hard-and-fast distinction between revealed and natural religion, between faith and reason, which, though it dominated the thought of the later medieval centuries, is notably absent from St. Anselm's pages; and in so doing it seriously misrepresents both the latter's conception of faith and his conception of reason. The faith or belief which he considers must precede rational understanding is very far from being a blind acceptance of tradition; rather is it such an inward laying hold of God as, following upon the gracious act by which God lays hold of us, forms the secret of the deepest personal religion. And St. Anselm never regards it as the function of reason to *justify* this saving faith in God; but only to *understand* it —a very different and far more modest office. 'I have written the following treatise', he declares in the Preface, 'in the person of one who . . . seeks to understand what he believes.' Similarly in his *Cur Deus Homo* he sets out by saying: 'Just as the right order of going (*rectus ordo*)

[1] Chapter I.

135

requires that we should believe the deep things of Christian faith before we presume to subject them to rational discussion, so also it seems to me negligence *not* to do our best, after we are confirmed in faith, to understand what we believe. . . . By the prevenient grace of God I believe myself so to hold the faith of our redemption that, even were I unable by any exercise of reason to understand what I believe, yet nothing could possibly avail to tear me away from the strength of it.'[1]

The notion that it is the function of reason to justify a belief already held on grounds of mere authority, though it cannot be attributed to St. Anselm, may, however, be fairly attributed to that later thinker whose way of arguing for God's existence most reminds us of St. Anselm's, namely, Descartes. It cannot indeed be said of Descartes, any more than of St. Anselm, that he deemed it proper that belief in God should supervene for the first time upon the successful completion of an argument for His existence. Cartesian doubt, whether of God or of the external world, does not imply the suspension of all practical belief; it is rather a nicely balanced mental gymnastic by which full practical commitment is made to consort with a theoretical open-mindedness. Descartes accordingly tells us that he continued to believe in God even while subjecting His existence to Cartesian doubt. But, unlike St. Anselm, the later thinker does seem to rely upon a rigid distinction between reason and revelation and to understand faith as the acceptance of authority. 'I revered our theology', he writes, 'and aspired as much

[1] Chapter I.

as anybody else to reach heaven; but having been taught as a thing well assured that the way thither is no less open to the most ignorant than to the most learned, and that the revealed truths which lead to it are above our understanding, I did not dare to subject them to the impotence of my reasonings'[1]—a backwardness of which the robust-minded Archbishop of Canterbury shows no sign. So Descartes assures us that in embarking upon his course he 'placed in reserve the truths of faith which have at all times been first in my belief'.[2] Whether these statements can be taken as entirely ingenuous is a question which need not concern us here.

If then we return to St. Anselm, we find ourselves confronted with the contention that the office of the so-called theistic proofs is never to induce belief but only and always to provide us with a better understanding of a belief already firmly held. That this has in most cases been the *actual* order of events it is impossible to deny; and therefore we are bound to admire St. Anselm's *honesty*. But that it should be regarded as the *proper* order of events may appear more difficult to believe; and we may accordingly have our doubts as to St. Anselm's *wisdom*. For it will be said that the conclusion must, *vi termini*, come at the end of the argument and not at the beginning of it.

Yet it is just here, I am convinced, that we are mistaken and that St. Anselm is right—or is at least leading us in a right direction. There is undoubtedly a field of truth-seeking in which the knowledge of the conclusion comes only at the end of the argument, namely, the field of

---

[1] *Discours de la Méthode*, Part I.   [2] Ibid., Part III.

mathematics and the natural sciences. But there is another field of which something like the reverse seems to be true, and this includes the objects of theological discourse. Here, indeed, we seem to come upon one of the characteristic differences that distinguish what the Germans call the *Geisteswissenschaften* from the mathematical and natural sciences; and if this be true, then we have been seriously misled by the Cartesian tradition which sought to model all philosophy on the geometrical pattern— *more geometrico*, according to the already quoted phrase of the Cartesian Spinoza. 'I took delight above all in mathematics', writes Descartes in the little tractate which launched the Cartesian movement and the tercentenary of whose publication at Leyden we are this year[1] celebrating, the *Discourse on the Method of Rightly Conducting One's Reason and of Seeking Truth in the Sciences*, 'on account of the certitude and evidence of its reasonings; but I had not yet discovered its true use, and, thinking that it was of service only to the mechanical arts, I was astonished that, its foundations being so firm and so solid, no loftier structure should have been built upon them. Whereas on the other hand I compared the writings of the ancient pagan moralists to very superb and magnificent palaces which were built on nothing better than sand and mud. . . .'[2] Yet I am convinced that it is the ancient pagan moralists who were right and Descartes who was wrong, and that it is the old Socratic and Aristotelian method that must here be followed rather than this new mathematical one. In the ethical classroom we may, for

[1] 1937.   [2] Part I.

instance, often discuss the question *why* honesty or un-selfishness is obligatory, but I am sure we ought never to discuss the question *whether* they are obligatory. The moment we essay so to do we are lost in unreality and (what is the same thing in this region) dishonesty. For we already *know* that they are obligatory; and if we did not know this in advance, then we should never know it at all. So again in our discussions in the philosophical classroom concerning solipsism and our knowledge of other minds, it is never an open question *whether* other minds exist; rather do we set out from the knowledge of their existence, and our inquiry is only as to the precise nature of the process whereby this knowledge has been obtained. Again, in the theological classroom it is, I believe, never a genuinely open question whether God exists or even (to mention one other example) whether He is One; the open question is only as to the nature and grounds of our already existing belief in His Being and in His unity. Here again I find Mr. Collingwood's state-ment more clarifying than any other. He contrasts what he calls the irreversibility of mathematical argument with the reversible character of philosophical argument. 'This irreversibility', he writes, 'is a necessary feature of exact science; it can only argue forwards from principles to conclusions, and can never turn round and argue back-wards from conclusions to principles. . . .'[1] With this, he goes on, is to be contrasted 'the Socratic principle that philosophical reason leads to no conclusions which we did not in some sense know already. Every school of

[1] Op. cit., p. 153.

philosophical thought has accepted this principle, recognizing that philosophy does not, like exact or empirical science, bring us to know things of which we were simply ignorant, but brings us to know in a different way things which we already knew in some way'.[1] 'Establishing a proposition in philosophy, then, means not transferring it from the class of things unknown to the class of things known, but making it known in a different and better way. . . . Here philosophical thought shows a contrast with that of the exact sciences. Our knowledge that the square on the hypotenuse is equal to the sum of the squares on the other two sides depends (I speak for myself) on the proof. There are cases, as I have already remarked, in which we intuitively apprehend the conclusion without the proof; but normally the proof is our only source of assurance that the conclusion is true. In philosophy this is not so; we know this normally without any proof at all; and the service which the proof does for us is not to assure us that it is so, but to show us why it is so, and thus enable us to know it better.'[2]

---

[1] Op. cit., p. 161.

[2] Ibid., p. 161 f. I quote this from Mr. Collingwood; but that his statement does but clarify for me something that had long been in my own mind will be seen from the following sentences taken from the section entitled 'The Limits of Deductive Proof' in my *Interpretation of Religion*, published five years before Mr. Collingwood's book: 'To begin with, it must be clearly understood that formal deduction is always, to a greater or less extent, of the nature of an afterthought. . . . But there is none the less a vast difference between different fields of our knowledge in respect of the extent to which this ideal limit is approached. We come closest to it in pure mathematics; where, for instance, it is true that mankind actually did not know that the three angles of any triangle are together equal to two right angles until a Greek geometer arrived at that conclusion by a syllogistic

But now there is a question which we must put. If our faith in God's existence does not itself rest on argument, then how can the construction of an argument lead, as St. Anselm says it does, to the correct *understanding*[1] of that faith?

The only possible answer would be to claim that the argument which was afterwards hit upon was no more than the clear explication of a logical structure which had been already 'implicitly' contained in the mental process by which the faith was originally acquired; and though St. Anselm never explains himself on this point, it would appear that something of the sort was in his mind. Such a claim could not indeed be made for those traditional proofs on which St. Thomas Aquinas and the later school-men were afterwards to place their sole reliance; nor did it occur to St. Thomas or to any one else to make it. It is quite certain that it was *not* the discovery of design in nature that led the rude forefathers of our race to believe in the existence of gods, just as it is certain, in the words of 'Rabbi' Davidson, that 'The Hebrew thinker came down from his thought of God upon the world; he did not rise from the world up to his thought of God. . . . The world did not suggest to him an idea hitherto strange, that of the existence of God.'[2] So far from the idea of

process. . . . Now there can be no doubt that in this respect religion lies at the very other end of the scale from such a field of knowledge as geometry. . . . And this fact alone should have been a sufficient reason against the Cartesian attempt to model a constructive theology on the thirteen books of Euclid's *Elements*—as indeed Pascal clearly saw in Descartes' own time' (p. 359 f.).

[1] St. Anselm uses both *intelligere* and *comprehendere*.

[2] Op. cit., p. 32.

141

God having first arisen in men's minds as an hypothesis to explain the world, it is only a very small number of peoples who have ever advanced so far as to believe that the God or gods of whose existence they were so firmly persuaded were in any sense responsible for bringing the world into being. And though it is now far more difficult than it was a few years ago to make confident statements about the development of Hebrew religious thought, the experts do still seem to be more or less agreed on the fact that the Israelites firmly believed in Jehovah for hundreds of years before they came to regard Him as the Creator of the world and of man—and this in spite of the impression that is not unnaturally caused by the order in which the Old Testament documents appear in our canon. If any of these facts are true, then clearly it cannot be claimed that the Thomistic arguments for God *per ea quae facta sunt* bear any relation to the process by which the knowledge of God actually came into the world.

With reference, however, to the very different line of proof on which St. Anselm relied—and which St. Thomas rejected—the claim might possibly be put forward that it represents only a more detailed explication of the very process of thought which is implicitly present in faith itself. This is true even of the line of proof suggested in his *Monologion*, but it is still more true of the famous 'ontological argument' which it was the aim of the *Proslogion* to expound. For, unlike the traditional arguments, the ontological argument is not an attempt to rest the knowledge of God on some prior knowledge, namely, knowledge of the world; rather does it regard the knowledge of God as itself *a priori*, finding in God Himself the premiss from which His existence must be deduced; and it attempts only to show that to form the conception of God in our minds is already to believe in His reality.

It might therefore be supposed that, just as the intention of St. Anselm's proof is confessedly not to lead us to believe in God, so also its intention is not to show us *why* we already believe in Him, but only to convince us *that* we already believe in Him. That this was St. Anselm's own reading of his proof does not, however, appear. And it is just here, as I believe, that we must part company with him. *No* proof of God's existence can help us to understand our faith in Him, or can in the last resort do anything but hinder such understanding, *if* it be true that it is not by a process of inference that our faith has actually been reached. And that I believe this to be true I have already sufficiently indicated. It is not as the result of an inference of any kind, whether explicit or implicit, whether laboriously excogitated or swiftly intuited, that the knowledge of God's reality comes to us. It comes rather through our direct personal encounter with Him in the Person of Jesus Christ His Son our Lord.

CHAPTER IV
THE URGENT PRESENCE

§ 13

'NEXT to the foolishness of denying God, certainly the greatest is that of proving Him.' That sentence, coming as it does from a distinguished theologian of the Barthian school, serves to indicate how far the thought of our own time is tending to move away from the standpoint of the old apologetic. In his book *Science and the Modern World* Professor Whitehead complains that 'for over two centuries religion has been on the defensive, and on a weak defensive'.[1] Yet there is, I believe, no mistake of the past that we are to-day more anxious to retrieve.

In the foregoing chapter our contention was that our knowledge of God is not inferential in character and that the attempt to reach God by means of argumentation is therefore wrong in principle. Yet if the full extent of this wrongness is to be clear to us, there still remains something to be said.

Let us consider what we do when we reach any reality by means of argument. Clearly what we do is to deduce this reality from some other reality which is already known to us. This other and previously known reality may in its turn have been deduced from a third reality our knowledge of which was again prior to our knowledge of the second. Yet if we are to avoid the fallacy of an infinite regress, this process of constantly falling back upon prior premises must somewhere reach its term in some reality which is known to us in some more direct

[1] p. 270.

way than by deduction from something already known. Not all our thinking can be discursive; it must contain some element of immediacy. Otherwise it would be 'as if one should say that in building a wall every brick must be laid on the top of another and none directly on the ground'.[1] Kierkegaard found another figure. 'In order to sew', he was fond of saying, 'we must first have a knot in the thread.' There must be some reality by which we are directly confronted—some reality which we know, not because we know something else first, but rather as itself the ground of our knowledge of other things. This does not mean that this prime reality either originally was or conceivably could be known to us in isolation from all other realities—for there is nothing that can be known by us out of relation to all other things; it means only that in being known together with other things it is known and recognized as their ground.

What then is this prime reality? The common-sense answer will perhaps be said to be that it is the material world. Dr. Samuel Johnson, that paragon of common sense, who has indeed been described[2] as 'the most abnormally English creature God ever made', thought that in order to refute Bishop Berkeley's apparent subjectivism he did not need to *prove* the existence of such things as stocks and stones—it were enough to bump the doubter's head against one, meeting him in this way not with argument but with direct confrontation! And whether or not this view can fairly be attributed to

[1] G. F. Stout, *Studies in Philosophy and Psychology*, p. 308.
[2] I think by Professor G. M. Trevelyan.

present human common sense, I suppose we may admit that it is the view to which we are predisposed by our inheritance from our simian ancestors whose one standard of reality was doubtless the solid wooden branch of the tree to which they clung. Now it cannot be said that a view of this kind necessarily lies behind all the theistic argumentation that finds its starting-point in the world of nature and argues 'from nature to God'; for Plato, who initiated such argumentation, was himself the protagonist in the refutation of this view. But the tradition of such argumentation has been kept alive, not by the true followers of Plato (the Neoplatonists and other Platonic idealists), but rather by the Aristotelians and Thomists, both of whom were essentially realists. Aristotle, indeed, in opposing Plato's idealism, seems to have prided himself upon, precisely, his common sense. He 'had perfect faith in the ultimate validity of the data of the senses', and 'the whole doctrine of the illusory character of the world of sense is foreign to the Aristotelian system'.[1] In this respect, as in many others, St. Thomas was undoubtedly an Aristotelian rather than a Platonist. His contention that 'the only road which can lead to a knowledge of the Creator must be cut through the things of sense' plainly goes together with his conviction that our primary knowledge is only of the things of sense.

Modern philosophy, however, started with a different view. Descartes found it only too easy to doubt the reality of the things of sense and, far from taking them

[1] P. H. Wicksteed, *The Reactions between Dogma and Philosophy illustrated from the Works of St. Thomas Aquinas*, pp. 8, 11.

as the prime reality from the certainty of which all further certainties must be derived, he found himself falling back from them upon some ulterior certainty which should guarantee their own reality. This ulterior certainty he found in God. Apart from his trust in God, he explains, he would have found it entirely possible to suppose that the things of sense were no more real than the things seen in dreams. 'But after having realized that there is a God, and since at the same time I realized also that all things depend on Him, and that He is no deceiver, and inferred from this that all that I clearly and distinctly perceive must of necessity be true, it is now impossible, by the presentation of a reason to the contrary, to make me doubt again anything once believed to be true, even though the reasons for its truth are no longer in my mind, provided only that I remember to have clearly and distinctly apprehended it at the time. . . . And thus I very clearly realize that the certitude and truth of all science depends only on the knowledge of the true God, inasmuch as, before I knew Him, I could not perfectly know anything else whatever.'[1]

Yet for Descartes the certainty of God, though thus ulterior to that of the things of sense, was not the ultimate certainty, for he found that it too was capable of being doubted in its turn. The only ultimate certainty which he found it quite impossible to doubt was the existence of *himself*; since, as he said, the very act of doubting implied at least the existence of the doubter. For the existence of God, therefore, some sort of proof must still

[1] *Méditations*, v.

be found; and since it could not be a proof from nature, which had already been shown to be knowable only through the knowledge of God, it must be a proof which finds its premiss only in René Descartes and the ideas present in his mind; it must, that is to say, be a proof which starts not from *res extensa* but from *res cogitans*. St. Thomas's proofs are accordingly set aside in favour of something that closely resembles the Anselmic proof which St. Thomas had condemned.

It appears, then, that from one point of view the Cartesian revolution registered a very real gain. God was now recognized as a Reality who more directly confronts us than do the things of sense, and our certainty of Him became prior to the certainties of science rather than dependent upon them. This changed emphasis dominated the history of continental thought throughout the whole of the seventeenth and eighteenth centuries. It is the foundation of the whole idealistic tradition in modern philosophy—a tradition the immensely liberating influence of which, as over against every acknowledgement of the primacy of the things of sense, most of us will be very ready to recognize. In English thought this changed emphasis is reflected in the philosophies alike of Berkeley and of Locke. 'I say, then,' writes the latter, 'that we have the knowledge of our own existence by intuition; of the existence of God by demonstration; and of other things by sensation.'[1] Hence, as he goes on to say, it is from the intuitive knowledge of our own existence that the demonstration of God's existence must

---

[1] *Essay Concerning Human Understanding*, iv. 9, § 2.

begin. 'To show, therefore, that we are capable of knowing, i.e. being certain, that there is a God, and how we may come by this certainty, I think we may go no further than ourselves and that undoubted knowledge we have of our own existence.'[1]

But if there was gain in the Cartesian revolution, there was also very serious loss. For when, after retreating from nature to God, Descartes went on to retreat farther from God to Descartes, it is doubtful whether he was not after all setting himself in worse case than he was before. So long as the material world remained the ground of all certainty, one was at least confronted with objectivity, even if it were the wrong kind of objectivity. But in finding the ground and type of all certainty in his own existence, Descartes was shutting himself up within his own subjectivity. In the last analysis, then, he was but exchanging the materialistic predicament for what has come to be called the ego-centric predicament. He did indeed, as we have seen, think himself able to extricate himself from this ego-centric predicament by means of his Ontological Argument, by which he thought himself able to pass from his own existence to the existence of God. Yet few have been found to agree that he did so successfully; and from that day to this, modern philosophy has never been entirely rid of the nightmare of this dreadful solitude that surrounded its birth. More and more the conviction has been borne in upon us that, if we may allow ourselves the Irishism, the only way to get out of the ego-centric predicament is never to get into it.

[1] *Essay Concerning Human Understanding*, iv. 10, § 1.

To some extent the mistaken nature of the Cartesian starting-point has been recognized ever since Kant, though it cannot be said that Kant himself succeeded in being free from its influence. Our post-War generation of thinkers has, however, gone much farther, so that there is hardly one of them who does not regard it as typifying, and in large part also originating, the fundamental error of modern European thought; the latest of such critics being the Archbishop of York, one of whose Gifford Lectures was entitled 'The Cartesian Faux-Pas', and who spoke of the day when Descartes hit upon his *Cogito ergo sum* as 'perhaps the most disastrous moment in the history of Europe'. Exactly where, then, did Descartes's mistake lie? It lay, surely, in supposing that the consciousness of self preceded the consciousness of the not-self, or could remain after the consciousness of the not-self had disappeared. The truth is that only in the knowledge of what is other than myself am I able to rise to the knowledge of my own existence at all. Descartes agreed that the very existence of his doubt implied the existence of himself who doubted; what he should have argued was that it implied the indubitable presence to his experience of something not himself which should be his standard for judging whether other things were doubtful or not doubtful; for it is clear that if he had no sense of reality he could have no disposition to doubt. Psychologically speaking, it is certain that the consciousness of self cannot precede the consciousness of other selves. A single human individual reared in isolation from society could develop no self-consciousness at all, but would remain for ever like Tennyson's 'baby new to earth and sky' who 'has never thought that "this is I" '.[1] Nothing, therefore, could be more topsy-turvy than the idea that our human certainty begins in the knowledge of ourselves and afterwards, taking that as its premiss, proceeds to the knowledge of what is not ourselves.

Yet it was no mere error of formal logic of which Descartes was guilty, nor again was it merely an error of technical psychological analysis. Rather was he misled into these formal errors by the very temper of the age in which he lived. In his selection of his own selfhood as the type and ground of all certainty we cannot but see the reflection of that general humanistic bias which characterized the thought of the post-Renaissance period. And now, living as we do in an age which has been spoken of as 'the end of the Renaissance', we find ourselves even more profoundly repelled by the *humanism* of the Cartesian starting-point than by the subjectivity of it— though indeed the two are very closely interrelated. It is error enough to be surer of oneself than of one's friends; but it is a still greater error to be surer of oneself than of God.

[1] *In Memoriam*, xliv.

§ 14

THE witness of all true religion is that there is no reality which more directly confronts us than the reality of God. No other reality is nearer to us than He. The realities of sense are more obvious, but His is the more intimate, touching us as it does so much nearer to the core of our being. God's approach to us in Christ is the closest approach that is ever made to the inmost citadel of our souls—

> The hold that falls not when the town is got,
>   The heart's heart, whose immurèd plot
>   Hath keys yourself keep not![1]

'Behold, I stand at the door and knock', says Christ; and though many knockings are more obtrusive, none is so patient or in the last resort so ineluctable. God alone is omnipresent. His is the only claim that is always with us and never lets us go. 'Whither shall I go from thy spirit? or whither shall I flee from thy presence? If I ascend up into heaven, thou art there: if I make my bed in Sheol, behold, thou art there. If I take the wings of the morning, and dwell in the uttermost parts of the sea; Even there shall thy hand lead me, and thy right hand shall hold me. If I say, Surely the darkness shall cover me; even the night shall be light about me. Yea, the darkness hideth not from thee, but the night shineth as the day: the darkness and the light are both alike to thee.'[2]

---

[1] Francis Thompson, *A Fallen Yew*.   [2] Psalm cxxxix.

I am sure that, in proportion as we are honest with ourselves, we shall all have to confess to this haunting Presence. It has been with us from our youth up, and we know that it will be with us to the end. No other challenge that has ever reached us has been so insistent or so imperious. You and I have often tried to evade it; we have done many things in its despite; sometimes, when its demands were most inconvenient, we have tried to pretend that it had no right to be there at all. But in the bottom of our hearts we have never been able to doubt its right. We have always known that there is no other sovereign right but this, and no other 'totalitarian' authority. We are surrounded by many glaring realities that occupy the foreground of our consciousness and make all sorts of claims on our attention and allegiance; but we have always known that only one obligation is absolute and one imperative categorical. Moreover, you and I have always known that this claim that was being made upon us was being made upon us for our *good*, and that in yielding to it lay our only true salvation. Even when we most tried to escape from it, we still knew that our deepest weal lay in obedience. We knew that it was sovereign Love that was here constraining us and claiming us for its own; and we knew that in the last resort it was something that was being *offered* us rather than asked of us—and that what was being asked of us was only that we should accept the offer. So when men gazed upon the figure of the Crucified Christ, they were conscious of all the rebuke it held for them, all the condemnation of their sin, all the rigour and austerity of its demands;

but behind all they knew most certainly that 'herein was love'. 'For God sent not his Son into the world to condemn the world; but that the world through him might be saved.'[1]

I have already spoken of the Kantian revolution as that next following upon the Cartesian in the order of modern thought. In Kant's Critical Philosophy there is a most valuable recovery of the fundamental truth upon which I have been dwelling, yet Kant was still too much in bondage to the humanistic tradition, and particularly to the eighteenth-century stratum of that tradition, to let it appear in anything but a sadly curtailed and impoverished form. Kant's great rediscovery was that of the Primacy of the Practical Reason, as he called it. It is not in the realm of sense, he believed, that we are all really in touch with absolute objective reality, and certainly not in the realm of the supersensible objects of scientific and metaphysical speculation, but only in the realm of the practical claim that is made upon our wills by the Good. Ultimate reality meets us, not in the form of an object that invites our speculation, but in the form of a demand that is made upon our obedience. We are confronted not with an absolute object of theoretical knowledge but with an absolute obligation. We reach the Unconditional only in an unconditional imperative that reaches us. There is here, as it seems to me, most precious and deeply Christian insight. But where Kant erred, and where his eighteenth-century education was too much for him, was in his analysis of this experience into mere

[1] John iii. 17.

respect for a law. The eighteenth century had its own very remarkable greatness, but it also had its obvious limitations—limitations which could not, in fact, be better exemplified than in this proposal to make *law* at once the primary fact in the universe and the prime object of our *respect*. Something of this respect for law we can still conjure up as we stroll through the well-ordered palace and gardens of Versailles, or again as we wander at will through the equally well-ordered couplets of Alexander Pope's poetry; yet between us and both of these experiences stands that Romantic Revival which, in spite of all its regrettable extravagances, has taught us a delight in *fera natura* of which we shall never again be able entirely to rid ourselves. The reduction of the spiritual life of mankind to the mere respectful acceptance of a formula was, in fact, the last absurdity of the eighteenth century. It is no mere formula with which the sons of men have ever found themselves faced as they approached life's most solemn issues, but a Reality of an altogether more intimate and personal kind;[1] and respect or *Achtung* is hardly an adequate name for all the fear and the holy dread, the love and the passionate self-surrender, with which they have responded to its presence. We must indeed do Kant the justice of remembering that he discovered a process of reasoning which, as he thought, justified him

[1] 'For no law, apart from a Lawgiver, is a proper object of reverence. It is mere brute fact; and every living thing, still more every person exercising intelligent choice, is its superior. The reverence of persons can be appropriately given only to that which itself is at least personal.'—Archbishop Wm. Temple, *Nature, Man and God*, p. 255. Dr. Temple italicizes the whole passage.

in envisaging this moral law in a more concrete way as the commandment of a holy God. In this way something of the true spiritual life of mankind seems to find its way back into his scheme. Yet the loop-hole by which it is allowed to enter is so narrow that little or nothing of the rich reality of it succeeds in getting through. Kant's religion remained to the end a mere legalistic moralism *plus* a syllogism that allowed him to conceive of an eighteenth-century Legislator behind His eighteenth-century law. 'Thus', as—to take only one example—he himself most cogently concluded, 'the purpose of prayer can only be to induce in us a moral disposition. . . . To wish to converse with God is absurd: we cannot talk to one we cannot intuit; and as we cannot intuit God, but can only believe in him, we cannot converse with him.'[1]

Now it seems to me that it is precisely such a sense of *converse* with the Living God as Kant thus clearly saw to be excluded by his own system that lies at the root of all our spiritual life. That life finds its only beginning in the revelation to our finite minds of One whose transcendent perfection constitutes upon our lives a claim so sovereign that the least attempt to deny it awakens in us a sense of sin and shame; and thus is initiated the sequence, ever extending itself as the revelation of the divine nature becomes deeper and fuller, of confession, repentance, forgiveness, reconciliation, and the new life of fellowship. *There is no other spiritual sequence than this.* What we now so glibly speak of as our moral consciousness is an abstraction obtained by stripping this sequence of

---

[1] *Lectures on Ethics*, translated by L. Infield, p. 99.

most of its characteristic and all its deepest features, until at last it has the appearance of a process that goes on entirely within ourselves rather than a converse that takes place between ourselves and Another. The notion of a 'morality' that can exist by itself apart from God and religion is a typical product of eighteenth-century humanistic rationalism. It made its first full-dress appearance just before that century was ushered in—in the *Inquiry Concerning Virtue and Merit*, published by the third Earl of Shaftesbury in 1699 (to be republished in 1711 as part of the famous *Characteristics*). Here was invented that notion of a special 'moral sense' which played so dominant a part in the thought of the century, especially after its further development by Francis Hutcheson. It is well known that the works of Shaftesbury and Hutcheson were read by Kant at an early period of his life, influencing him profoundly; and though he was soon led by the stern Protestantism of his upbringing to revolt against their emphasis on feeling and to find his own foundation for morals rather in the pure reason, yet he never ceased to share their strong prejudice against what he called a 'theological ethic'. Thus has the great prestige of his name been lent to the very modern heresy of a moral life that is apart from the worship of God.[1]

[1] So far as Kant's campaign against a theological ethic was directed against the nominalist and voluntarist variety of theological ethic which, strongly entrenched as it was in the German Protestant tradition, was the variety most familiar to himself, and which made the moral law dependent on the Divine Will as distinct from the Divine Reason, I believe it to have been fully justified and most salutary in its results. But so far as it was a campaign against *all* theological ethic, I believe it to have been disastrously wrong.

In spite of all this, however, we are bound, as I have already said, to see in Kant's philosophy a most valuable recovery of the fundamental truth that Absolute Reality, instead of being reached speculatively by means of deduction from the data of sense, is revealed to us directly in the form of an Absolute Obligation. This means that what is revealed to us is not theoretical knowledge but practical guidance, and that what is asked of us in return is not intellectual assent but willing obedience. Here is grasped, as I believe, a most important truth which has profoundly influenced the thought of the last hundred years and which is coming to influence the thought of our own time more profoundly still. 'What does it want with us', asks Dr. Martin Buber in that little book of his to which I shall be referring in the next chapter as a minor classic of the thought of our time, 'what does it desire of us, this Meaning of our Life that is revealed and yet concealed? Not to be explained by us—that is beyond us—but only to be *done* by us. . . . Every revelation is a call and a vocation.'[1]

Nevertheless this truth, as it stands, is only half a truth. It is impossible to rest finally in this sharp dichotomy between knowledge and guidance, between understanding and obedience, since it is only by knowledge that we can be guided, and since we cannot obey what we do not understand. In the obligation that is revealed to us some element of knowledge must be implicitly contained. So much was clearly recognized by Kant himself. He opposed, and rightly opposed, that intellectualistic notion

[1] *Ich und Du*, pp. 127, 133.

of revelation which made it consist in *orthodoxy*, that is, in quasi-scientific truths or ideas *about* God; he insisted that what was revealed to us was rather a practical way of salvation; but he knew well that this way of salvation contained in itself a true mode of the knowledge of God, and he knew also that the right name for this mode of knowledge was *faith*.

Where he erred was in his understanding of the relation of the faith to the guidance. He taught, as we have seen, that the guidance is originally revealed to us in the form of a self-evidencing *law*—a mere obligation detached, as it were, from Him who lays the obligation upon us; and that the knowledge of Him who thus obliges us is afterwards reached as an inference from the felt nature of the obligation. We, on the other hand, have argued that the Source of the obligation is Himself directly revealed to us and that it is in this vision of His glory and His holiness that our sense of obligation is born. It is *His* perfection that rebukes us; it is *His* love that constrains us. Hence it is no mere law that is revealed to us, but a living Person, and what we call the moral law is but an abstraction which our limited and limiting minds make from the concreteness of the living Glory that is revealed. Even of our human saints and heroes M. Bergson has said, 'Ils n'ont pas besoin d'exhorter: ils n'ont qu'à exister; leur existence est un appel.'[1] Certainly we can say this of God. He challenges us by being what He is, not by exhorting us to be what He is not, or by issuing commands which His own nature does not obey. God and His Word are

[1] *Les deux sources de la morale et de la religion*, p. 30.

one. It is Himself that His revelation reveals. 'The Word was God.'[1] This is excellently expressed by the Archbishop of York in a passage of his Gifford Lectures which well retains, and no less well supplements and corrects, the deep insight of Kantianism. 'The real acceptance of such revelation', he writes, 'is not only intellectual assent; it is submission of will. And this must be submission to the revelation as personally received, not only to the record of it as received by some one else. Every revelation of God is a demand, and the way to knowledge of God is by obedience. It is impossible to have knowledge of God as we have knowledge of things, because God is not a thing. We can only know a person by the direct communion of sympathic intercourse; and God is personal.'[2]

Moreover, as against Kant, we must here lay further stress on a point which has already been touched upon. What we have most fundamentally to do with in religion is not a demand that is being made upon us but a gift that is being offered to us. A demand is indeed made, but it is a demand that we should accept a gift. '*Da quod iubes, et iube quod vis.*' We are asked, not to do anything in our own strength, but to let God do something for us. We are summoned, not to save ourselves, but to accept Christ's salvation. It is true that while we continue to give no heed to the summons the glory of the gift will remain hidden from us, and we shall be aware only of the demand. 'The Cross is the revelation of the love of God

---

[1] John i. 1.
[2] *Nature, Man and God*, p. 254. The whole passage is italicized. Cf. the closely related passages quoted from Dr. Temple in § 4 above.

only to those who have first stood under it as judgment.'[1]
He who refuses God's love can only know His wrath.
This is what is meant by the saying that some men have
just enough religion to make them desperately miserable.
In this sense, then, it is quite true that religion is known
as Law before it is known as Gospel, and to this extent
Kant was justified in his contention that the awareness
of the moral demand precedes the apprehension of God
by faith. Yet it must be insisted that the demand made
upon us is recognized by us from the beginning as a
demand that we should accept a gift. In essence, as we
must all bear witness, it is not a demand that we should
assert our wills, but a demand that we should surrender
them; a demand, not to remake our lives, but to allow
them to be remade. So, as Dr. Brunner puts it in a fine
treatment of this matter, at the heart of the *Aufgabe* there
is the *Gabe*—at the heart of the task there is the gift. 'God
claims us for His love,' he writes. 'This is His command.
. . . It is the command of One who gives before He
demands, and who only demands something from us in
the act of giving Himself to us.'[2]

Kant, therefore, though well aware that God, in
making a demand upon us, is at the same time offering
us a true knowledge of Himself, is far from fully understanding the relation of this demand to this knowledge,
of this imperative to this indicative, or (in the crude way
that we have come to express it) of 'ethics' to 'religion'.

[1] Reinhold Niebuhr in his speech before the Oxford Conference on
Church, Community, and State, July 1937.

[2] *The Divine Imperative* (English translation of *Das Gebot und die
Ordnungen*), p. 116.

Yet when he goes on to descant on the impossibility of turning this knowledge, given with a view to our salvation, into a scientific account that will satisfy our speculative curiosity, he is again, as I believe, saying something of the very first importance, something also which the development of thought between his day and ours has gone very far to confirm. 'We have indeed a knowledge of God,' he writes, 'but one that is given us only in a practical connection'; hence we must not 'make the attempt to stretch it out into a theoretical knowledge' or 'theory of supersensible realities', as do the 'pretended practitioners of natural theology' (*vermeinte natürliche Gottesgelehrte*).[1] This teaching is plainly very closely related to, and is no doubt in part the source of, that distinction between the detached thinking proper to scientific inquiry and the 'existential' thinking proper to religion which, under the influence of Kierkegaard, has found its way into so much of our post-War philosophy and theology; very closely related also to the further doctrine that when religious thinking ceases to be 'existential' it must, if it is not entirely to lose touch with reality, become 'dialectical', that is, be refracted in two opposite directions, each one of which is a necessary complement and corrective of the other; very closely related, once more, to the emphasis on the unknowableness of God, on the *Deus absconditus*, which is so striking a feature in the theology of Dr. Barth and his friends.

[1] *Kritik d. praktischen Vernunft*, *Werke* ed. Pr. Akad. d. W., Band V, p. 137. But this passage is, of course, merely one of very many in which the same thing is said.

15

THE position I am maintaining is that there is no reality by which we are more directly confronted than we are by the Living God. It has often been taught that it is not really necessary in the interests of personal religion to occupy such high ground. It has been thought sufficient to maintain that God is the ground of all being without going on to maintain also that He is the ground of all knowledge. It has been thought sufficient to say that He comes first in the *ordo essendi* but not in the *ordo cognoscendi*; that He is therefore *notior per se* but not *notior nobis*; or again that He is *prior simpliciter* but not *prior quoad nos* —which is of course but a translation of the Aristotelian distinction between what is πρότερον ἁπλῶς and what is πρότερον πρὸς ἡμᾶς. It has been justly pointed out that the attempt made in the various theistic proofs to deduce God's reality from the reality of other things does not make God's being derivative, but only makes our knowledge of Him derivative; and it has been held that to this latter derivation no proper exception can be taken, but that, on the contrary, it is in accordance with the facts of the spiritual life. God, it is said, is the first reality to exist but the last to be known.

This is the distinction which is relied on by Kant and by all Kantians—including, at least as regards one oftenquoted passage,[1] Albrecht Ritschl; and under the in-

---

[1] *Justification and Reconciliation*, vol. iii, English translation, p. 226 and footnote.

fluence of the Ritschlian Wilhelm Herrmann I was myself
inclined to rely upon it at an earlier stage in my theological reflections. But, as the scholastic forms of its
expression are themselves sufficient to indicate, it was
equally relied upon, long before the days of Kantianism,
by those natural theologians of the Middle Ages whom
Kant so much disliked, and above all by St. Thomas
Aquinas;[1] and it is now regarded as a necessary part of
Roman orthodoxy.

Now I am not myself so anti-Roman in sentiment that it
can ever be an entirely easy thing for me to find myself at
variance with an important tenet of medieval orthodoxy.
Yet it sometimes happens that, if only I am able to discover what were the influences leading to the adoption
of such a tenet, the measure of its authority seems to be
very palpably lessened. In the last chapter I set out very
fully St. Thomas's view that in this life we have no direct
knowledge of God but know Him only by causal and
analogical inference from the things of which we do have
direct knowledge. But we may now ask ourselves *why*
St. Thomas thought it necessary to adopt such a position.
The answer seems to be twofold. The first determining
factor is clearly his Aristotelian epistemology, which pre-
cludes him from believing that we can have direct knowledge of any existence that is not corporeal in nature so
as to be capable of being perceived by one or more of the
five senses. 'Aquinas', says Wicksteed, 'holds firmly to
the anti-mystic psychology of Aristotle as far as the
natural and earthly life is concerned,' so that it is only

[1] *Summa contra Gentiles*, i. 11.

after death, when our psychical natures are miraculously changed, that 'we may hope to gain some powers of direct perception of spiritual beings'.[1] It is very important to notice that the same psychological principles which thus preclude St. Thomas from allowing the possibility of a direct knowledge of God, preclude him also from allowing the possibility of a direct knowledge of our fellow men, or even of ourselves. Of our fellow men also it is true that we do not know at all what they are in themselves, but only know their *effects* on the material world. Their essence is no less completely hidden from us than is the essence of God. And so also is our own essence. Hereafter we may, acquiring new powers, become self-conscious, just as we shall become conscious of God; but meanwhile—so Wicksteed expounds St. Thomas—'it is a mistake to call the mind or soul of man "self-conscious". . . . We are conscious of the *operations* of our souls, for these we can observe and classify just as we can the operations of anything else. But the soul itself, as a being, out of whose nature all these operations follow, so that we could predict them because we know their source and cause—what do we know of that? Here on earth, then, we do not so much as know our own souls.'[2] The second determining factor in St. Thomas's view derives, however, not from Aristotelianism but from that other ancient tradition by which he was only less profoundly influenced, namely, Neoplatonism. It is well known that there is in all Neoplatonism, whether pagan or Christian, a strongly ag-

[1] Op. cit., pp. 651, xxii.   [2] Op. cit., pp. 366–7.

nostic strain. It teaches us that God is to be reached not so much by a progressive enrichment of our experience as by a process of abstraction, a progressive removal of limitations, a continual subtraction rather than addition, so that in the end we can discover much that He is not, but nothing that He positively is. Here, then, is the source of that theology of the *via negativa* which so dominated the Christian thought of the Middle Ages. 'By reason of His pre-eminence,' wrote John Scotus Erigena in the ninth century, 'God may not unjustly be spoken of as Nothing.'[1] The greatest transmitter of this Neoplatonism to the Middle Ages was undoubtedly the so-called Dionysius the Areopagite, whose Greek works, dating probably from the fifth century, Erigena translated into Latin. The influence of Dionysius partly reached St. Thomas through the treatises of the eighth-century systematizer John of Damascus, whom he is constantly quoting; but of its determinative nature there can be no doubt.

But now, if we share neither St. Thomas's Aristotelian epistemology nor his Neoplatonic absolutism, there would appear to be no particular reason why we should accept his view that our only knowledge of God is of an inferential and analogical character.

Furthermore, it must be remembered not only that for all the Christian Neoplatonists the *ideal* knowledge of God is precisely such a direct vision of Him as their agnosticism makes them believe to be normally denied

---

[1] *Deus per excellentiam non immerito nihilum vocatur*: quoted by W. R. Inge, *The Philosophy of Plotinus*, vol. ii, p. 112.

to us, but also that by no means all of them agree with St. Thomas that for the enjoyment of such knowledge we must necessarily wait for a future life. Erigena, it is true, goes even farther than St. Thomas in a negative direction, holding that no created being, not even the angels, can ever in any state of life, present or future, know God in His essential being. But there is in Medieval Platonism another strain, represented by St. Bernard, by Richard and Hugh of St. Victor, and above all by St. Bonaventure —while it had also been represented in an earlier century by St. Anselm—which teaches that some vision of God may be enjoyed even in this life, at the summit of the mystical ascent, and without miracle. It is indeed characteristic of the mind of St. Thomas that, standing midway between these two positions, he should draw an entirely hard and fast line between what is possible *in via* and *in patria*, holding that in this life there can (apart from miracle) be no vision at all, while it is the normal mode of knowledge among the blessed in the hereafter.

Moreover, as we already had occasion to note in the last chapter, St. Bonaventure goes farther still, thereby exposing himself to the criticism of St. Thomas. For he holds not only that the ecstatic experience of God is the crown of the religious life on earth, but also that *some* direct knowledge of God is native to every human soul prior to the construction of all arguments to prove His existence. Such arguments, he explains, may indeed be constructed, but they are never the real point of departure. God is indeed knowable to us through the things which He has made (*per creaturas*), but He is still more clearly known to us through His presence (*per praesentiam*) and in Himself (*quantum est de se*).[1] He is 'most truly present to the very soul of man and is in that fact already knowable'.[2] He is indeed far enough removed from us in the order of being, yet He is directly present to us in the order of knowledge. Hence he expresses His agreement with St. Anselm's contention that it is impossible for a man to conceive of God as non-existent. But what then, it will be asked, of the difference between such knowledge of God as we have on earth, and the vision of Him that is reserved for the blessed in heaven? That difference is in the last resort as present to the mind of St. Bonaventure as to that of St. Thomas, yet it is noteworthy that the former is less troubled than is the latter by the scriptural use of the language of vision in respect of certain experiences that have been enjoyed by men on earth. His pilgrim spirit never forgets that 'now we see through a glass darkly (*per speculum in aenigmate*), but then face to face'; but, remembering also the second half of the same Pauline verse, that 'now we know in part (*ex parte*)',[3] he appears much less concerned than is Aquinas to draw the line sharply as between two diverse *kinds* of seeing. Even in our earthly communion with God there is something of the substance of beatitude. It can never indeed be more than an earnest, a fragmentary foretaste of that which is to come, yet it too is in its measure an enjoy-

[1] *Sententiae*, Dist. III, Pars I, Art. I, Quaest. I.

[2] *Quaest. disp. de Mysterio Trinitatis*, ix. 1. *Deus praesentissimus est ipsi animae et eo ipso cognoscibilis.*

[3] 1 Corinthians xiii. 12; cf. Vulgate.

ment of the real presence of God. *In patria*, we shall know Him perfectly through His presence, but even *in statu viatoris* we can know Him through His presence *semiplene*—'half-fully'.[1] In all this St. Bonaventure may be said to be representing the Franciscan tradition as against the Dominican tradition which is represented by St. Thomas.

As has been said, however, it is St. Thomas rather than St. Bonaventure who has ever since determined the direction taken by Roman orthodoxy. The view that in this life we can know God directly, or otherwise than inferentially, has come to be spoken of within that Church as *ontologism* and as such has always been condemned. Ontologism is not the same thing as acceptance of the Ontological Argument, but there is a natural connexion between the two, and St. Thomas condemned them both alike.[2]

Twice during the nineteenth century the Holy Office thought it necessary to repeat its condemnation of 'the errors of the ontologists'. This was mainly in connexion with the views of the two Italian philosophers, each of them in other respects a good catholic and Thomist, namely Vincenzo Gioberti (1801–52), all of whose works were finally placed on the Index, and Antonio Rosmini-Serbati (1797–1855), founder of the order of the Brethren of Charity (known in Italy as the Rosminians), and forty of whose opinions were condemned by Leo XIII in 1887. Since the promulgation of these decrees the lovers of St.

[1] *Sententiae*, Dist. III, Pars I, Art. I, Quaest. III.
[2] *Summa contra Gentiles*, i. 10–11.

Bonaventure have sought to maintain that the Seraphic Doctor was not guilty of the errors of ontologism,[1] yet Rosmini and his followers had always been in the habit of appealing to his deliverances. It is perhaps worth while to set down here the seven ontologist propositions condemned by Pius IX in the decree of the Holy Office dated 18th December 1861.

'1. The immediate knowledge of God, at least so far as it is habitual, is essential to the human intellect, so that without it nothing can be known, since it is itself the intellectual light.

'2. That being which we apprehend in all things and without which we apprehend nothing is the Divine Being.

'3. Universals, objectively considered, are not objectively distinct from God.

'4. The innate notion of God, as Being without qualification, involves every other knowledge *eminenti modo*, so that by means of it we implicitly know every living being in whatsoever respect it is knowable.

'5. All other ideas are but modifications of the idea by which God is apprehended as Being without qualification.

'6. Created things are in God as a part within a whole, not indeed in a formal whole, but in an infinite and uncompounded whole, in that He sets what are, as it were, His parts outside Himself without in any way dividing or diminishing Himself.

'7. Creation is to be explained as follows: By that

[1] e.g. *The Franciscan Vision*, by Father James (1937), pp. viii, 7.

173

same special act by which God apprehends and wills Himself as distinct from a determinate creature such as man, He produces that creature.'[1]

There are, indeed, in these seven propositions, as in the systems of philosophy from which they are extracted, many things that merit emphatic rejection—which, however, is something different from pontifical condemnation. Yet, I believe, there is also in them an element of truth, which we shall do right to defend against the Thomist doctrine of the priority of the things of sense. When the Holy Office condemns ontologism, it is really intending to condemn the view that the knowledge of God is *innate*, part of a fixed and given constitution with which the human species was initially endowed; and that indeed is a view to be rejected. But what ought to be affirmed in opposition to it is not the inferential nature of our knowledge of God, but rather the *continual invasion* of our life by His holy Presence.

In opposing ontologism Dr. Hubert Box thus states what he believes to be the true as well as the orthodox position: 'An act of divine faith is an act by which one believes whatever God has revealed on God's authority. It is, therefore, obvious that we cannot make an act of divine faith before we have been convinced by reason that God exists and that He has spoken. . . . The conviction that there is a God can only be reached by reasoning which, when fully thought out, is tantamount to a meta-

---

[1] See Denzinger-Bannwart, *Enchiridion Symbolorum*, 21st edition (1937), p. 465 f. For a defence of Rosmini against the charge of ontologism see T. Davidson, *Compendium of the Philosophical System of Antonio Rosmini-Serbati* (London, 1891), p. 338 f.

physic. .... The ultimate basis of religious conviction is reasoning, whether it take the rough and ready form known as common sense, or appear as an elaborate argumentation which not only is metaphysical, but is recognized as such.'[1] As against such an analysis I believe that ontologism has something true to contribute; and as against it I have myself already maintained that revelation essentially consists not in the communication of truths about God but in the self-revelation of the divine Personality, the truths about Him being abstracted by ourselves from the concrete reality with which we thus become acquainted, and our knowledge of His existence being given in and with the revelation rather than guessed at in advance of it.

It is not enough, then, to acknowledge God as the most real of all realities. We must acknowledge Him also to be, of all realities, that by which we are most directly and intimately confronted. There is, indeed, a sense in which God's reality is a question which I, as one of His creatures standing in His holy presence, am not *allowed* to discuss. How could the thinking concerned in such discussion be really 'existential' in character? How can I, who in this very moment that I write am conscious of a demand being made *now* upon my life by God and His Christ, stand aside from the situation of responsibility thus created in order coldly to debate the question whether the God who thus claims me so much as exists? Even if the demand made of me were con-

[1] *The World and God; The Scholastic Approach to Theism*, by Hubert S. Box, with a preface by the Rev. M. C. D'Arcy, S.J. (London, 1934), p. 32 f.

ceived as no more than a human demand; if, for example, as I now write, some fellow men were to rush into my study, inconveniently disturbing the train of my thought by the announcement that I was needed outside to help a passer-by who had fallen among thieves; would it be permitted me to reply, 'Your demand is very tiresome. But I am not yet sure that you exist. The solipsists *may* be right. Before acceding to your request, let me first see whether I can demonstrate your existence to my own satisfaction'? The comic absurdity of such a response is not greater than would be its wickedness if it should lead to even the least delay in my readiness to do what was demanded. It seems, then, that I am not allowed to take the solipsist hypothesis seriously—in spite of its having been solemnly discussed by many philosophers. And neither, I am convinced, am I allowed to take the atheistic hypothesis seriously, though that also has been the object of much discussion in the schools. Just as the unreality and impropriety of all arguments for the existence of other minds lie in the fact that they all start from a possible solipsism, so the unreality and impropriety of the theistic arguments lie in the fact that they all start from a possible atheism. They start from a situation in which God is not yet. But there is no such situation, if it be true that in every moment I am called upon to obey His holy will—and that I have been so called upon from the beginning. Atheism is not a prior situation which theism must presuppose, but a situation which itself pre-supposes the theism of a world already challenged by the revelation of God in Christ.

More and more, then, the thought of our time seems to be converging towards such a view as that expressed by Professor Tillich when he writes: 'Arguments for the existence of God presuppose the loss of the certainty of God. That which I have to prove by argument has no immediate reality for me. Its reality is mediated for me by some other reality about which I cannot be in doubt, so that this other reality is nearer to me than the reality of God. For the more closely things are connected with our interior existence, the less are they open to doubt. And nothing can be nearer to us than that which is at times farthest away from us, namely God. A God who has been proved is neither near enough to us nor far enough away from us. He is not far enough, because of the very attempt we have made to prove Him. He is not near enough, because nearer things are presupposed by which the knowledge of Him is mediated. Hence this ostensibly demonstrated subject is not really God.'[1]

[1] From an article on 'The Religious Situation in Germany To-day', in *Religion in Life*, vol. iii, no. 2 (New York, 1934), p. 167.

16

YET, though we are more directly and intimately confronted with the presence of God than with any other presence, it does not follow that He is ever present to us *apart* from all other presences. And, in fact, it is the witness of experience that only 'in, with and under' other presences is the divine presence ever vouchsafed to us. This aspect of the matter was referred to at the begining of this chapter, but must now be more fully investigated.

I believe the view to be capable of defence that no one of the four subjects of our knowledge—ourselves, our fellows, the corporeal world, and God—is ever presented to us except in conjunction with all three of the others. Here, however, we need only concern ourselves with the fact that God does not present Himself to us except in conjunction with the presence of our fellows and of the corporeal world.

Taking the second point first, it seems plain that the consciousness of God is never given save in conjunction with the consciousness of things. We do not know God through the world, but we know Him with the world; and in knowing Him with the world, we know Him as its ground. Nature is not an argument for God, but it is a sacrament of Him. Just as in the sacrament of Holy Communion the Real Presence of Christ is given (if the Lutheran phrase may here be used without prejudice) 'in, with and under' the bread and wine, so in a wider sense the whole corporeal world may become sacramental to

178

us of the presence of the Triune God. The conception of a sacramental universe thus expresses the truth that lay behind St. Thomas's natural theology, while being free from the errors in which the latter became involved. No writer has done more to clarify our thought on this matter than Baron von Hügel. 'Necessity of the Thing-element in Religion' is not only the title of a section in his greatest work,[1] but a constant theme in all his works. 'Spirit', he tells us, 'is awakened on occasion of Sense.'[2] The knowledge of God, he insists, is not during this life given to us in its isolated purity, but only through 'the humiliations of the material order'.[3] The knowledge of God which we have on earth is of a kind that we cannot conceive to exist apart from some knowledge of things.

But it is equally certain that all our knowledge of God is given us 'in, with and under' our knowledge of one another. This means, first, that the knowledge of God is withholden from those who keep themselves aloof from the *service* of their fellows. It means that 'He that loveth not knoweth not God',[4] whereas 'If we love one another, God dwelleth in us'.[5] And this is indeed a blessed provision by which God makes my knowledge of Himself pass through my brother's need. It means, second, that only when I am in *fellowship* with my fellow men does the knowledge of God come to me individually. It means the necessity of the Church and the rejection of religious individualism. It gives the true

[1] *The Mystical Element in Religion*, 2nd edition, vol. ii, pp. 372 ff.
[2] *Essays and Addresses*, 2nd series, p. 246.
[3] See the chapter on 'The Natural Order' in M. Nédoncelle's *Baron Friedrich von Hügel*.   [4] 1 John iv. 8.   [5] 1 John iv. 12.

sense of the Cyprianic formula, *extra ecclesiam nulla salus.*
'For where two or three are gathered together in my
name, there am I in the midst of them.'[1] Such was the
promise; and its fulfilment came when the disciples 'were
all with one accord in one place' and the Spirit 'sat upon
each of them'.[2] It means, third, the necessity of history.
There is a necessary historical element in all religion, for
we know of no religion that is not dependent on tradition; but Christianity is plainly an historical religion in
the fullest possible sense. The Christian knowledge of
God is not given to any man save in conjunction with
the telling of an 'old, old story'. Therefore it means,
lastly, the necessity of Christ, God incarnate in the flesh.
'For there is one God, and one mediator between God
and men, the man Christ Jesus; who gave himself a
ransom for all, to be testified in due time.'[3] The service
of others, the fellowship with others, and the historical
tradition in which I stand are all media that lead me to
the Mediator, and the Mediator leads me to God. And
all this mediation is part of God's gracious purpose in
refusing to unite me to Himself without at the same time
uniting me to my fellow men—in making it impossible
for me to obey either of the two great commandments
without at the same time obeying the other. This understanding of the relation of faith to history is one which
has been greatly clarified for us by Dr. Gogarten and
other writers of his school.[4] It is finely summarized by

[1] Matthew xviii. 20.   [2] Acts ii. 1-3.   [3] 1 Timothy ii. 5-6.
[4] See especially F. Gogarten, *Ich Glaube an den Dreieinigen Gott: eine
Untersuchung über Glauben und Geschichte* (1926); *Glaube und Wirklichkeit*
(1928).

Dr. Brunner: 'However inconceivable for us the miracle of the Incarnation may be, yet God lets us in some measure learn why his revelation happens precisely thus and in no other way. It is the wisdom and the goodness of the ruler of the world that he has revealed himself once for all at a particular place, at a particular time. Inasmuch as God, so to speak, deposits his gift of salvation at this one historical place, he compels at the same time all men who wish to share in this gift to betake themselves to this one place, and there to meet each other. . . . It is as if God had used a stratagem by so revealing himself that he can only be found when we find our brother along with him, that in order to find him we must let ourselves be bound to our brother. Only in the bond which unites me to the historical fellowship of my fellow believers—to be more exact, in the fellowship of those who believed before me—is my faith possible. . . . I must, so to speak, submit to becoming myself a member of the fellowship, if I wish to enter into relation with God. God will not bind me to himself on any other terms than these, that he binds me at the same time to my brother.'[1]

Clearly, then, the immediacy of God's presence to our souls is a mediated immediacy. But I must now do what I can to resolve the apparent self-contradictoriness of this phrase.

What I must do is to ask myself how the knowledge of God first came to me. And here I can only repeat what was said in the opening pages of this book: unless my

[1] *God and Man*, English translation, p. 126 f.

analysis of my memory is altogether at fault, the knowledge of God first came to me in the form of an awareness that I was 'not my own' but one under authority, one who 'owed' something, one who 'ought' to be something which he was not. But whence did this awareness come to me? Certainly it did not come 'out of the blue'. I heard no voice from the skies. No, it came, without a doubt, from what I may call the spiritual climate of the home into which I was born. It came from my parents' walk and conversation. At the beginning it may have been merely the consciousness of a conflict between my mother's will and my own, between what I desired and what she desired of me. Yet I cannot profess to remember a time when it was merely that. I cannot remember a time when I did not already dimly know that what opposed my own wilfulness was something much more than mere wilfulness on my mother's part. I knew she had a right to ask of me what she did; which is the same as to say that I knew that what she asked of me was right and that my contrary desire was wrong. I knew, therefore, that my mother's will was not the ultimate source of the authority which she exercised over me. For it was plain that she herself was under that same authority. Indeed, it was not only from my parents' specific demands on me that this sense of authority came to me but from the way they themselves lived. Clearly they, too, were under orders, and under essentially the same orders. I cannot remember a time when I did not already know that what my parents demanded of me and what they knew to be demanded of themselves were in the last resort one and the same demand, however different might be its detailed application to our different situations. I cannot remember a time when I did not know that my parents and their household were part of a wider community which was under the same single authority. Nor again, can I recall a time when I did not know that this authority was closely bound up with, and indeed seemed to emanate from, *a certain story*. As far back as I can remember anything, my parents and my nurses were already speaking to me of Abraham and Isaac and Jacob, of Moses and David, of God's covenant with the Israelites and of their journey through the wilderness, of the culmination of the story in the coming of Jesus Christ, God's only Son, whom He sent to earth to suffer and die for our salvation; and then of the apostles and martyrs and saints and 'Scots worthies' whose golden deeds brought the story down to very recent days. And I knew that that story was somehow the source of the authority with which I was confronted. I could not hear a Bible story read without being aware that in it I was somehow being confronted with a solemn presence that had in it both sweetness and rebuke. Nor do I remember a day when I did not already dimly know that this presence was God.

It was, then, through the media of my boyhood's home, the Christian community of which it formed a part, and the 'old, old story' from which that community drew its life, that God first revealed Himself to me. This is simple matter of fact. But what I take to be matter of fact in it is not only that God used these media but that in using them He actually did reveal Himself to *my* soul.

For what I seemed to know was not merely that God had declared His will to my parents and that they in their turn had declared their will to me, but also that through my parents God had declared His will to me. The story told me how God had spoken to Abraham and Moses and the prophets and apostles, but what gave the story its power over my mind and imagination and conscience was the knowledge that 'in, with and under' this speaking to these others of long ago He was also now speaking to myself. That God should have revealed Himself to certain men of long ago could not in itself be of concern to me now; first, because, not being myself privy to this revelation, I could never know for sure whether it were a real or only an imagined one; second, because mere hearsay could never be a sufficient foundation for such a thing as religion, though it might be well enough as a foundation for certain other kinds of knowledge; and third, because the revelation would necessarily lack the particular authorization and relevance to my case which alone could give it power over my recalcitrant will. What is it to me that God should have commanded David to do this or that, or called Paul to such and such a task? It is nothing at all, unless it should happen that, as I read of His calling and commanding them, I at the same time found Him calling and commanding me. If the word of God is to concern me, it must be a word addressed to me individually and to the particular concrete situation in which I am standing now. This insight into what we may perhaps venture to call the necessary 'here-and-nowness'—the *hic et nunc*—of revelation is one which has emerged very strikingly from recent theological discussions. Kierkegaard's doctrine of the 'existential moment'[1] has been a potent influence on many writers; but I need perhaps mention only Dr. Eberhard Grisebach's elaborate demonstration in his book called *Gegenwart*[2] that our sole touch with reality is in the present, the past and the future being alike unreal except so far as they are contained in the present moment.

In a letter to M. de Beaumont, Rousseau once asked, 'Is it simple, is it natural, that God should have gone and found Moses in order to speak to Jean Jacques Rousseau?' No, it is far from simple; but what right have we to assume that truth is simple? And as to whether it is natural, have we any knowledge of what would be natural in such a region of experience apart from the witness of the experience itself? We have to take experience as we find it—though that apparently was what Rousseau was refusing to do. And especially we have to face the fact that we have here to do with an experience of an entirely unique kind, its uniqueness lying precisely in this conjunction of immediacy with mediacy—that is, in the fact that God reveals Himself to me only through others who went before, yet in so doing reveals Himself to me now.

This is, indeed, a mysterious ordering of things. Yet I would not be understood as trying to surround it with

[1] See especially his book *Der Augenblick* (1855).
[2] *Gegenwart, eine Kritische Ethik* (1928).

any spurious air of mystery. Mysterious though it be, it is a mystery with which all men have some degree of acquaintance. It was not *only* in the Bible stories that I was met in my youth with this peculiar conjugation of past and present. Other tales of later days were told me, and in them the same Presence seemed to be speaking to me something of the same word. Were this Presence and this word in *every* tale I was told? I think not. There were, for instance, fairy stories; and they, though they absorbed my interest and caught my imagination, seemed to have nothing to say to me, nothing to do with me. And of some other stories the same thing was true. The stories that had Presence in them for me, though they were by no means always Bible stories, were somehow of a piece with the Bible stories. Usually, indeed, they were Christian stories, and as such were definitely derivative from the Bible history. But even when that was not the case, if they had Presence in them at all, it was the same Presence as met me in the Bible. And to this day all the history that has Presence in it for me, all the history that has anything to say to me, all of the past through which I am addressed in the present, is centred in the story of the Incarnation and the Cross. All that history has to say to me is somehow related to that; and no story that was entirely out of relation to that could have any present reality in it for me at all. Every story is either B.C. or else A.D.; and that not in mere date but in its very essence; logically as well as chronologically. Indeed, the same story may be chronologically A.D. yet logically B.C., such as stories of noble deeds done within the Christian era by men of other lands whom the knowledge of Christ has not yet reached. Such deeds seem to me to look forward to the Incarnation and the Cross rather than back to them, so that the doers of them are still living as it were under the Old Dispensation. Perhaps these truths of experience on which I have been dwelling have never received better intellectual formulation than in Professor Tillich's doctrine of *die Mitte der Geschichte*, where it is taught that history can have meaning only if it have a centre, and that for the Christian that centre is necessarily Christ. 'In dealing with the philosophy of history', he writes, 'it is impossible to avoid the Christological problem. History and christology belong to one another as do question and answer.' 'Instead of the beginning and end of history determining its centre, it is its centre that determines its beginning and end. But the centre of history can only be the place where is revealed the principle that gives it meaning. History is constituted when its centre is constituted, or rather—since this is no mere subjective act—when such a centre reveals its centrality.'[1]

The question may now be raised whether a story that has no Presence in it and no word to speak to us really partakes of the true nature of history at all; that is, whether anything can be history for the Christian which does not stand in relation to Christ as its centre. When Dr. Barth insists, as he does so often, that in history in general there is no revelation, since revelation interrupts

---

[1] *Religiöse Verwirklichung* (1930), pp. 111, 116. The essay from which I quote is translated in *The Interpretation of History* (1936), pp. 242 ff., but I have not followed this somewhat unsatisfactory translation.

history at a single point rather than informs it throughout, he is obviously thinking of history as something past and done with. Christ, he says, comes vertically into history and He *alone* reveals God; the history into which He comes does not reveal God *at all*. Thinking of history in this way, the Barthian theologians always oppose 'the Christ of Faith' to 'the Christ of History'. History, they say, cannot give you the truth about Christ; only faith can do that. I believe this dichotomy to be radically mistaken. I believe that a historiographer who writes without faith produces *bad history*. I believe that faith is quite essential to sound historiography. And I believe Professor Tillich's doctrine of Christ as the centre round which all history arranges itself to be altogether profounder than the Barthian attempt to set the rest of history in contrast with Christ. To Professor Tillich history is nothing dead and desiccated, 'the presence of the past in the present' being essential to its very nature, so that he can say that in ancient Greek thought 'there is no conception of the world as history, even though history as a report on the complex of human movements and as a pattern for politicians be not lacking to it'.[1] A similar view is eloquently defended by Dr. Gogarten, to whose treatment of this whole matter I have already acknowledged my debt. 'However one may try to solve it', he writes, 'and however one may alter its form in so doing, the problem of history is fundamentally the problem of the presentness of the past. Were the past merely past, as it is in the case of all natural events, there would be no

[1] Op. cit., p. 112.

188

such thing as history but only an unhistorical present—
and indeed not even that. For there can be a real present
only where there is something past that becomes present.'
'History is something that happens in the present.'[1] Such,
surely, is the right way of it. *It is only in the conception
of history as something that happens in the present that the
apparent contradiction in our doctrine of a mediated immediacy
can be reasonably resolved.*

It will perhaps help to draw the discussions of this
chapter to a conclusion if we now ask ourselves how far
this doctrine of a mediated immediacy is in accord with
certain deliverances of Martin Luther touching mediation
which have been made much of by the Ritschlian and
Barthian theologians. In a hundred passages scattered
throughout his works Luther warns us in almost identical
terms against indulging in 'curious speculations concerning the divine majesty'. 'We must abstain', he writes in
one place, 'from the curious searching of God's majesty,
which is intolerable to man's body, and much more to
his mind. "No man", saith the Lord, "shall see me and
live." ... But true Christian divinity ... setteth not God
forth unto us in His majesty. .... It commandeth us not
to search out the nature of God; but to know His will
set out to us in Christ.'[2] The Ritschlians were right in
finding a close affinity between this strain in Luther's
thought and the Kantian doctrine that we can attain no
knowledge of God of a kind to satisfy our speculative
curiosity regarding His nature, but only a practical know-

---

[1] *Ich Glaube an den Dreieinigen Gott*, pp. 71 f., 83.
[2] *Commentary on Galatians*, Ch. I, v. 3. English translation of 1575.

ledge of His will for our lives. Nor can it reasonably be doubted that Kant himself was here influenced by his Lutheran inheritance. Both Kant and Luther teach that the true knowledge of God is given only in relation to problems of conscience, though they interpret the nature of the relation very differently. Sometimes, however, Luther seems willing to allow, as Kant would not have allowed, that the speculations of natural theology have a certain legitimate use of their own, if not exactly in 'true Christian divinity'. 'Whensoever thou hast to do therefore with the matter of justification, and disputest with thyself how God is to be found that justifieth and accepteth sinners . . . then know thou that there is no other God besides this man, Christ Jesus. . . . But apart from the matter of justification, when thou must dispute with Jews, Turks, Papists, heretics, &c., concerning the power, wisdom and majesty of God, then employ all thy wit and industry to that end, and be as profound and as subtle a disputer as thou canst; for then thou art in another vein. But in the case of conscience, of righteousness and life, . . . against the law, sin, death and the devil, or in the matter of satisfaction, of remission of sins, of reconciliation, and of everlasting life, thou must withdraw thy mind wholly from all cogitations and searching of the majesty of God, and look only upon this man Jesus Christ, who setteth himself forth unto us to be a Mediator. . . . This doing, thou shalt perceive the love, goodness and sweetness of God; thou shalt see his wisdom, power and majesty sweetened and tempered to thy capacity. . . .'[1]

[1] *Commentary on Galatians,* Ch. I, v. 3. English translation of 1575.

Luther and Kant, then, both warn us against trying to reach a knowledge of God by means of the speculative reason. But Luther sees deeper than Kant into the nature of the wrongness of this endeavour. To him our attempt to reach God by speculation is but one form of our attempt to satisfy Him by our own works; and his principle of *sola fides* carries with it the equal rejection of both attempts. Christ is the Mediator not only of our reconciliation with God but also of our knowledge of Him; though indeed the two are one, since the only knowledge of God offered us is a reconciling, a saving, knowledge. A speculative knowledge of God as He is in His naked majesty would not and could not save, but would rather terrify and destroy. A saving knowledge, a knowledge that meets our situation as regards conscience and justification and reconciliation, must be a *veiled* knowledge. Such a veiled knowledge is given us in Christ. There God appears not in His naked majesty but in His humiliation. There He appears as a *man*, clothed in the raiment of mortality. There He appears not in His own impassibility but in weakness, suffering, and crucifixion. In this sense the *Deus revelatus* is a *Deus velatus*, a *Deus absconditus*; the unveiled God is a veiled and hidden God. This part of Luther's doctrine has often been said to be self-contradictory, but it is so only verbally. The meaning is simply that the God who is shown to us is shown in a veiled form. 'For to this end he came down, was born, was conversant among men, suffered, was crucified and died, that by all means he might set forth himself plainly before our eyes, and fasten the eyes of our hearts upon himself, that he might thereby keep us from climbing up into heaven, and from the curious searching of the divine majesty.'[1]

The speculative attempt to reach God in His naked transcendence Luther called the *theologia gloriae*; the knowledge of God in His humiliation (as 'clothed with man's nature') and in the sufferings of the Cross he called the *theologia crucis*—'the theology of the Cross'. This terminology was first used by him in the Heidelberg Disputation of 1518, when he defended a number of striking theses before the Annual Chapter of the Augustinians. From these the following may be quoted:

'19. He is not worthy to be called a theologian who sees the invisible things of God as understood through the things that are made (Romans i. 20).

'20. But only he who understands the visible and further things of God through the sufferings and the Cross.

'21. The theologian of glory says that evil is good and good evil; the theologian of the Cross says that the thing is as it is.

'22. That wisdom which sees the invisible things of God as understood through His works altogether puffs up, blinds and hardens.'[2]

In defending the twentieth thesis he further said, 'Because men misused the knowledge of God gained from His works, God wished rather to be known from His sufferings and to reject that knowledge of the invisible

[1] *Commentary on Galatians*, Ch. I, v. 3. English translation of 1575.
[2] Luther's *Werke*, Weimar edition, vol. i, p. 354.

through the knowledge of the visible, so that those who worship Him not as manifest in His works might know Him as hidden (*absconditum*) in His sufferings. . . . It suffices and profits nobody to know God in His glory and majesty, unless he know Him also in the humility and ignominy of the Cross. . . . Therefore the true theology and knowledge of God are in Christ crucified.'[1]

It is quite plain that the 'philosophers' and 'doctors' against whom this polemic is directed are the scholastic theologians. When Luther condemns the *theologia gloriae*, he is condemning precisely the kind of natural theology practised by St. Thomas—the attempt to reach God from 'the things which are made'. So far, then, Luther's criticism of the *theologia gloriae* corresponds exactly to our own criticism of Thomism. Some of the Barthian theologians, in reviving the use of this phrase, have understood it to mean a theology such as we can properly possess only in the state of glory, that is, a theology based on the direct vision of God. But, as we have had abundant occasion to note, a theology of glory in *this* sense, far from being practised by St. Thomas, was utterly abhorrent to him. His teaching was that all our knowledge of God is indirect and mediate, and that the immediate knowledge of God proper to the state of glory is completely impossible to us in our earthly condition. The *Deus velatus* and *Deus absconditus* were his phrases long before they were Luther's. There is nothing that he is fonder of quoting than the sentiment of Dionysius that *impossibile est nobis aliter lucere divinum radium nisi varietate*

---

[1] *Werke*, ed. cit., vol. i, p. 362.

sacrorum velaminum circumvelatum—'it is impossible that the divine radiance should ever shine upon us except as wrapped in a variety of sacred veilings'. What Luther really has in mind when he speaks of the theology of glory is not the knowledge proper to the saints in *their* state of glory but the knowledge of God in *His* naked glory and majesty. A recent writer says, 'Our knowledge of God is entirely mediate, and we must hold fast to the *media* which He has given us. This is the *theologia crucis* which Luther opposes to the *theologia gloriae* of the scholastics and all who presume to seek an immediate knowledge of God.'[1] But the scholastics, or at least the orthodox tradition of scholasticism to which Luther was more opposed than to any other, did *not* seek an immediate knowledge of God. Their mistake was of the opposite kind; they made our knowledge of God altogether *too* indirect and mediate, making it merely inferential in character; and they differentiated *too* sharply between the knowledges possible *in via* and *in patria*. The fact is that there is an immediacy about Luther's knowledge of God which is lacking in that of St. Thomas. The Thomist view is that we reach the knowledge of God through the knowledge of things other than God. The Lutheran view is rather that God reveals Himself to us directly, but in a veiled form. Here is one further passage from Luther— a passage especially interesting from its reference to the Presence of Christ 'in, with and under' the sacramental elements. 'God does not reveal Himself except in acts and in the Word, since these can in some way be grasped.

[1] George S. Hendry, *God the Creator* (1937), p. 93.

The rest of what belongs to deity cannot be grasped or understood as it is. . . . For our nature is so deformed by sin, so corrupted and destroyed, that it cannot know or comprehend naked deity for what it is. Therefore wrappings (*involucra*) are necessary. It is unwholesome to dispute much concerning God before time and outside of time, because that is to desire to comprehend naked divinity, the naked divine essence. Because this is impossible God wrapped Himself up in acts and in certain forms, as to-day He wraps Himself up in baptism, absolution, etc. . . . Therefore it is fanaticism to argue concerning God and the divine nature apart from the Word and some wrapping, as do all the heretics who discuss God with the same security as they do a pig or a cow. . . . But those who wish to reach God without such wrappings strive to climb heaven without ladders (that is, without the Word); therefore they perish, oppressed by majesty which they try to grasp in its nakedness, and are destroyed.'[1] We must, however, again remind ourselves of the scholastic denial that we can know God *per se*, and especially of the most insistent scholastic denial that we can know Him in His *essentia* or essential nature (as He is for Himself). If Luther is forgetting this, what he says is beside the point. But one further important difference there is between Luther and Aquinas, namely that for the former, as for St. Augustine,[2] it was the sinful corruption of human nature that rendered impossible the naked vision of the divine essence, whereas for the latter it was the original

[1] *Lectures on Genesis, Werke,* ed. cit., vol. xlii, pp. 9–11.
[2] Cf. A. L. Lilley, *Religion and Revelation,* pp. 24, 36.

constitution of human nature itself—so that even an un-fallen human knowledge of God must have been only inferential in character.

From all this it would appear that the type of mediation which we have been concerned to reject would have been emphatically rejected by Luther also, and that the type of mediation which Luther is concerned to defend is the same as we ourselves have defended.[1] When Luther affirms that Christ is the Mediator of the knowledge of God, he does not mean that we argue from Christ to God; he means that it is in Christ that we see God. We see Him veiled and humiliated, but it is nevertheless God that we see. The kind of directness for which we have contended in our knowledge of God is thus not at all interfered with, but is rather implemented, by the fact of Christ's mediatorship. This is what I have tried to express in the conception of a mediated immediacy. In

---

[1] This does not mean that I am prepared, as are apparently the Barthians, to defend all that is implied in Luther's doctrine of the *Deus absconditus*. I am not. There are aspects of his 'Christocentricity' which endanger a full understanding of what is implied in the doctrine of the Trinity. Nor must we make the affirmation that 'God is known to us only in His humiliation, in His sufferings and in the Cross', in such a way as to do injustice to our true knowledge of the divine impassibility. There is here a curious diffi-culty in Luther's teaching. If God is known to us only in His humiliation, then how do we know that apart from this humiliation His attributes are those of blinding glory and majesty? Yet there is nothing of which Luther seems more sure than of this latter. Moreover, it seems to me wrong to say that in Christ we see only a God who suffers, whereas apart from Christ we have somehow a knowledge of a God who suffers not. The glory and impassibility of God are no less revealed in Christ than are His pity and sympathy. There is in the figure of Christ a majesty, a serenity, an impassiveness, as well as a lowliness and a Passion. If we were here concerned with a complete criticism of Luther's theology, all this would be very important.

Christ we know God not by argument but by personal acquaintance. In Christ God comes to us directly. We must not understand our Lord's mediatorship in such a way as to forget the words, 'I and my Father are one'[1] or 'I am in the Father and the Father in me'.[2] Nor is there, as it seems to me, any reason to avoid altogether the language of vision. 'No man hath seen God at any time', but 'He that seeth me seeth him that sent me',[3] and 'If ye had known me, ye would have known my Father also; and from henceforth ye know him, and have seen him. . . . He that hath seen me hath seen the Father; and how sayest thou then, Shew us the Father?'[4]

Nor again can we follow St. Thomas in drawing his hard and fast distinction between the knowledge of God that is possible to us as *viatores* and the knowledge which is given to the blessed *in patria*. We have here as much to learn from the Seraphic as from the Angelic Doctor. Bonaventure's phrase that in this life we see God with the same kind of seeing as do the saints in glory, but only *semiplene*, half-fully, may seem too bold, yet such teaching is nearer the truth than the other.

> The streams on earth I've tasted
> More deep I'll drink above.[5]

St. Thomas defines that 'Those who see God are said to have eternal life',[6] and denies that even a beginning of such seeing is possible to us now. The New Testament, however, is by no means so rigidly futurist in its

---

[1] John x. 30.   [2] John xiv. 11.   [3] John xii. 45.
[4] John xiv. 7, 9.   [5] Mrs. Cousin's 'The Sands of Time are Sinking'.
[6] *Summa Theologica*, Pars I, Q. 10, Art. 3.

eschatology. There is in it, as is more and more coming to be recognized, a strong strain of 'realized eschatology', according to which even in this life the saints have already some foretaste of the glory that is to be revealed. For the fullness of eternal life we must indeed wait until the veil be lifted, but even now we may have some *arrhabo*, some earnest of what it means. Alike St. Paul and St. John know how to speak of eternal life, of the Kingdom of God, and even of resurrection, as something which, by way of foretaste, can be enjoyed now. 'The Kingdom of God', says St. Paul, 'is . . . righteousness and peace and joy in the Holy Ghost.'[1] 'Who hath delivered us from the power of darkness', he says again, 'and hath translated us into the kingdom of his dear Son.'[2] 'If ye then be risen with Christ, seek those things which are above.'[3] And St. John says, 'We know that we have passed (μετα-βεβήκαμεν) from death unto life, because we love the brethren.'[4] 'Verily, verily, I say unto you, He that heareth my word, and believeth on him that sent me hath ever-lasting life, and . . . is passed (μεταβέβηκεν) from death unto life. Verily, verily, I say unto you, The hour is coming, and now is, when the dead shall hear the voice of the Son of God: and they that hear shall live.'[5] 'And this is life eternal, that they might know thee the only true God, and Jesus Christ, whom thou hast sent.'[6]

[1] Romans xiv. 17.   [2] Colossians i. 13.
[3] Colossians iii. 1.   [4] I John iii. 14.   [5] John v. 24 f.
[6] John xvii. 3. For a fuller treatment of the presentness of eternal life, see my book, *And the Life Everlasting*, pp. 207-11. For the New Testament evidence see C. H. Dodd, *The Apostolic Preaching and its Development* (1936), especially pp. 133-89.

CHAPTER V

THE OTHER WHO IS MOST NEAR

§ 17

THERE is no more hopeful element in the philosophy of our time than the reopening of the question of the nature of our knowledge of one another. At the end of every great period of its history thought seems to find itself in a sort of cul-de-sac, making it difficult to imagine in what direction further advance is to be looked for—beyond, of course, a certain increased refinement of detail. What is needed is the opening up of a new vista, but none is able to guess what such a vista might be. In the early years of the present century, prior to the outbreak of the Great War, many students both of metaphysics and of theology were conscious of a situation of this kind. We seemed to have gone about as far as we could go along the line we were then pursuing. If we now feel, as I think we do, that we are out in the open once again, and on the way to fresh discovery, it is undoubtedly to the re-emergence of the problem of *other mind* that we owe one important part of our deliverance.

As is common in such cases, the new direction of thought cannot be traced to the influence of a single thinker. Rather do the various significant thinkers appear as themselves influenced by something that is new in the spirit of the age. Within the English-speaking world a remarkable anticipation is to be found in the already mentioned essay by Cook Wilson, which was first drafted as long ago as 1897. Some real anticipation also is to be found in a widely read American work, Professor

Hocking's *The Meaning of God in Human Experience*, published in 1912. Then, after the interruption of the War, there appeared in 1920 Samuel Alexander's Gifford Lectures on *Space, Time and Deity*, and Professor Webb's *Divine Personality and Human Life*. In 1930 Professor Webb followed up the latter with his British Academy Lecture on *Our Knowledge of One Another*. In two later lectures in the same series, some further contribution has been made to the discussion of the problem—by Professor Kemp Smith in his lecture of 1931 entitled *Is Divine Existence Credible?* and by Professor de Burgh in his lecture of 1935 on *The Relations of Morality to Religion*. To these there now fall to be added the relevant parts of the late Professor Bowman's *Studies in the Philosophy of Religion*, published posthumously in 1938, but completed in first draft as early as 1924.

It is, however, in the German-speaking lands that the new movement of thought has enjoyed its most remarkable development. In the background of this development we are indeed nearly always able to discern, though sometimes only dimly, the Danish figure of Sören Kierkegaard; yet it was only in the later years of the War, and under stress of its increasingly testing experiences, and for the most part on German soil, that this profoundly gifted eccentric began to come into his own after nearly a century of neglect. In 1921 the Austrian philosopher Ferdinand Ebner published his volume of 'pneumatological fragments',[1] which he had written during the

---

[1] *Das Wort und die geistigen Realitäten: pneumatologische Fragmente* (Innsbruck, 1921).

winters of 1918 and 1919, and in which the debt to Kierkegaard is fully acknowledged. In 1923 Dr. Martin Buber, who may be regarded as the spiritual leader of contemporary German Judaism, published his beautiful little book *I and Thou*, which is now available to us in Mr. Ronald Smith's English translation; but the first writing of this book dates also from the latter years of the War. In 1919 Dr. Barth published his veritably epoch-making commentary, *The Epistle to the Romans*, in which the influence of Kierkegaard is apparent and the new-emerging view of our knowledge of other mind is represented in the conceptions of the Word and of God as Subject. Dr. Barth and Dr. Buber must not be supposed to have had any influence on one another, yet their joint influence is very clearly seen in the writings of several Protestant theologians who went on at once to make further weighty contributions to the discussion; chief among them being Dr. Friedrich Gogarten. When Dr. Gogarten began to teach in the University of Jena in 1925, one of the professors of philosophy was Dr. Eberhard Grisebach, and it is not difficult to trace an affinity between the ideas which occupy the former in his writings published soon after that date[1] and the remarkable work published by the latter in 1928.[2] It is to Dr. Grisebach more than anybody else that we owe the working out of the *ethical* significance of the ideas made familiar to us by Dr. Buber. To Dr. Karl Heim, especially in the work the third and

[1] *Ich Glaube an den Dreieinigen Gott* (1926); *Glaube und Wirklichkeit* (1928).
[2] *Gegenwart, eine kritische Ethik.*

shortened edition of which has been translated into English by Professor Dickie under the title of *God Transcendent*, we owe an equally striking attempt to work out their *theological* consequences. As regards general epistemology, the influence of Kierkegaard may be found leading us in something of the same direction in the philosophies of Dr. Martin Heidegger and his disciple Dr. Löwith,[1] of Dr. Karl Jaspers, and—in France—of M. Jean Wahl.

The epistemology of the past had devoted its main energies to the analysis of two kinds of knowledge, our knowledge of ourselves and our knowledge of outside things—self-consciousness and our consciousness of the external world. Both in the medieval and in the modern period there is an astonishing paucity of reference to the problem of our knowledge of other selves, and anything that is said is mostly of a very perfunctory nature. The reason for this is that our knowledge of other selves tended to be regarded, not as a third kind of knowledge with a specific character of its own, but as reducible either to one of the other kinds or to a combination of the two. The view of St. Thomas Aquinas was indeed that there is fundamentally only *one* kind of knowledge, namely knowledge of the external world, and that both our knowledge of ourselves and our knowledge of others (including God) are of a dependent and secondary kind. But after the rise of modern philosophy it was commonly held that we have no less direct an awareness of our own existence than of the existence of things external to us,

[1] *Das Individuum in der Rolle des Mitmenschen* (1928).

and hence it came to be supposed that we reach the knowledge of other minds by means of an inference of which the major premiss is our awareness of our *own* minds and the minor our sensible perception of other *bodies*. I have direct introspective knowledge of the mind inhabiting my own body; by means of my senses I perceive other bodies which look and behave like my own; and I argue from analogy that these other bodies are likely to be similarly inhabited by minds. Writing as late as 1917 in his *Problems of the Self*, Professor Laird is still able to refer to this as 'the accepted theory'.[1] It is not easy, as has been said, to point to explicit statements of it, but we do find it fairly worked out in Bishop Berkeley's *Principles of Human Knowledge*. 'It is plain', we read there, 'that we cannot know the existence of *other spirits* otherwise than by their operations, or the ideas by them excited in us. I perceive several motions, changes, and combinations of ideas, that inform me there are certain particular agents, like myself, which accompany them and concur in their production. Hence the knowledge I have of other spirits is not immediate, as is the knowledge of my ideas; but depending on the intervention of ideas, by me referred to agents or spirits distinct from myself, as effects or concomitant signs.'[2] Berkeley was therefore able to claim that a God known only by inference from His effects in the world of nature was known in no more indirect a way than that in which we know

[1] pp. 24, 25.

[2] Op. cit., p. 145. The reader will keep in mind Berkeley's use of the term 'idea', which according to his philosophy is equivalent to 'thing perceived'.

our fellow men. 'Hence it is evident that God is known as certainly and immediately as any other mind or spirit whatsoever distinct from ourselves.'[1] The English bishop is at great trouble to persuade us that such analogical knowledge, whether of our friends or of God, is all that heart can desire; though, as we have seen, such a conclusion had already satisfied St. Thomas in thirteenth-century Paris, as it still appears to satisfy the Neo-Thomists of our own day. 'The non-philosopher', writes a recent exponent of Thomism, Dr. Hubert Box, 'hardly realises that the existence of other men is nothing more than an inference. We do not know by intuition that other persons exist. Our knowledge of their existence is not immediate but mediate. The inference by which we come to have the conviction that there is a God is only a little more difficult than that by which we come to be convinced that there are other persons beyond ourselves.'[2] Moreover, a similar view is championed by those contemporary Protestant theologians, like the late Dean Rashdall and Dr. F. R. Tennant, whom their adversaries would describe as being still too much in the 'rationalistic' tradition. 'There is no immediate or "intuitive" knowledge of God,' writes the former. 'Our knowledge is got by inference, like knowledge of our friend's existence.'[3] And the latter, having made the point that our knowledge of other selves is 'the outcome of analogical projection', goes on in similar terms to

[1] Berkeley, op. cit., p. 147.
[2] *The World and God: The Scholastic Approach to Theism*, p. 33.
[3] *Philosophy and Religion*, p. xiv.

deny that we have any direct or immediate knowledge of God. 'Knowledge of the self and the world', he holds, 'arise together and grow *pari passu*: knowledge of God is dependent on them.'[1]

Over against these statements let me now set the judgement of Cook Wilson: 'If we think of the existence of our friends; it is the direct knowledge which we want; merely inferential knowledge seems a poor affair. To most men it would be as surprising as unwelcome to hear it could not be directly known whether there were such existences as their friends, and that it was only a matter of (probable) empirical argument and inference from facts which are directly known. And even if we convince ourselves on reflection that this is really the case, our actions prove that we have a confidence in the existence of our friends which can't be derived from an empirical argument (which can never be certain), for a man will risk his life for his friend. We don't want merely inferred friends. Could we possibly be satisfied with an inferred God?'[2]

It is, however, not only the cheerlessness of the older view that has lately come home to so many of us but also its psychological untenability. The required inference by which, setting out from a solipsistic self-consciousness on the one hand and a consciousness of a merely corporeal externality on the other, the knowledge of other selves can be reached as a conclusion, is not really capable of precise formulation, however plausible it may be made

[1] *Philosophical Theology*, vol. i (1928), chs. v and xii; vol. ii (1930), ch. ix.　　　[2] *Statement and Inference*, vol. ii, p. 853.

to seem in a careless statement of it. It can, I believe, be refuted in no less than three ways: first, by showing that self-consciousness could not itself arise in advance of the recognition of other selves; second, by showing that our consciousness of the external world could not arise in advance of such recognition; and third, by showing that even if they could, the recognition of other selves could not arise out of them.[1]

Under the first of these heads something has already been said—in connexion with our criticism of Descartes. The solipsistic starting-point is at once ruled out by the fact that self-consciousness is so obviously a socially conditioned thing. Human personality, says Professor Ebner, 'always consists in the existence of the I in relation to the Thou'.[2] Or as Dr. Buber expresses it, even more elliptically, 'Ich werde am Du; alles wirkliche Leben ist Begegnung'[3]—'I come into being as over against the Thou; all real life is of the nature of encounter.' 'Ich bin durch dich',[4] says Dr. Gogarten—'Through thee I am.' 'For we do not begin', writes Professor Hocking, 'as solitary beings and then acquire community: we begin as social products and acquire the arts of solitude.'[5] Some of these

---

[1] Professor H. H. Price warns us that the champions of the newer view, which he rejects, often confuse the two questions of the *genesis* and the *justification* of our belief in other minds. (*Philosophy*, vol. xiii, no. 52, Oct. 1938, 'Our Evidence of the Existence of other Minds'.) But let it be clearly understood that we are here not in the least interested in any justification of this belief which is unrelated to its genesis. What we are investigating is the nature of our existing knowledge. We are asking why we believe in other minds, not why we ought to believe in them.

[2] Op. cit., p. 36. [3] Op. cit., p. 18.
[4] *Glaube und Wirklichkeit*, p. 57. [5] Op. cit., p. 299.

writers have understood this to mean that self-consciousness is preceded in time by the recognition of other selves.
The baby, it is said, is aware of its mother before it is
aware of itself—it says 'mama' before it says 'baby'. The
first words of Dr. Ebner's book are that 'The I is a late
discovery', and he goes on to say that it is formed 'by
abstraction from the Thou'. And Dr. Gogarten writes
in the context of the passage quoted above that 'the Thou
is always earlier than the I'. But this is not Dr. Buber's
view. According to him the I is not formed by abstraction from the Thou but from the I-Thou relation. The
prime word (*Grundwort*) is here 'the word-combination
I-Thou'. 'Prime words signify not things but relations.'[1]
'In the beginning is relation.'[2] 'Spirit is not in the I, but
between I and Thou.'[3] This seems to me the sounder
teaching, as it is certainly more in accordance with the
suggestion made in the last chapter, that no one of the
four objects of our knowledge—ourselves, our fellows,
the world of things, and God—is ever presented to us
save in conjunction with the other three. The baby may
say 'mama' before it says 'baby', but it is doubtful
whether it says 'thou' before it says 'I'.

Yet self-consciousness is no more obviously socially
conditioned than is our consciousness of the external
world. From the beginning that world presents itself to
us as a common world, a public world; and the ease with
which we distinguish it from the world of dreams is from
the beginning associated with the fact that the one is
public and the other private. The whole of Professor

[1] Op. cit., p. 9.   [2] Ibid., p. 25.   [3] Ibid., p. 49.

Heidegger's philosophy rests upon the realization that *alles Dasein ist Mitsein*—'all existence is co-existence'. 'The world is what I share with others.'[1] But Professor Hocking had already written, 'I do not first know my physical world as a world of *objects*, and then as a world of *shared* objects: it is through a prior recognition of the presence of Other Mind that my physical experience acquires objectivity at all. The objectivity of nature is its community.'[2] This means that the belief in the existence of other bodies cannot be prior to the belief in the existence of other minds; and that is the second reason why the analogical doctrine cannot be true.

But now if, for the sake of argument, we grant the possibility of a being who, while conscious both of himself and of the external world, was not yet conscious of other selves, it then becomes impossible to imagine how he could ever advance to this further consciousness. To one whose whole experience was dominated by the dualism of self as experiencing centre and a world experienced from that centre, what could be more essentially inconceivable than the existence of another centre of consciousness than his own? This is a thought that nothing could make him have, if he began by not having it. At most, writes Dr. Heim, he might perhaps come to 'regard the other physical appearance as a kind of soulless replica' of his own body.[3] 'That he should take this something other than himself', writes Dr. Webb, 'to

---

[1] *Sein und Zeit* (1927), p. 117.　　　　[2] Op. cit., p. 288 f.
[3] *God Transcendent* (English translation of 3rd edition of *Glaube und Denken*), p. 101.

be a reduplication of that which, . . . *ex hypothesi*, is essentially unique, the *solus ipse*, insistence on whose uniqueness for each subject is the very point of the doctrine which we are criticizing, this I cannot bring myself even to imagine.'[1] 'The idea of a foreign consciousness', writes Dr. Alexander, 'would be miraculous, if it were not based on a direct experience of it.'[2]

[1] *Our Knowledge of One Another*, p. 5.

[2] Op. cit., vol. ii, p. 33 n. Some writers, and notably Professor Stout in his Gifford Lectures on *Mind and Matter* (1931), put forward an alternative view of the nature of our knowledge of other minds which makes such knowledge inferential in character without basing it on *analogous* inference. It is not the *likeness* of certain bodies to our own that leads us to conclude that minds are associated with them, but the *responsive* character of their behaviour. 'The individual', writes Professor Stout, 'finds the first clue to the existence of other selves in the responsive behaviour of certain external objects as contrasted with the indifference of others. Behaviour is responsive when it is in a distinctive and spontaneous way relevant to the individual's own interests, his emotions and practical needs. . . . If when the baby was hungry, his bottle spontaneously approached his lips in the right position, and spontaneously went away again when his hunger was appeased, the bottle would be for him an embodied self, in spite of want of resemblance between him and it' (p. 303 f.). Such a view is indeed less remote from the truth than the other, and yet I am unable to accept it. Of course it is true that if the baby's bottle behaved in this spontaneous way, the baby would regard it as another self. And what is more, *he would be right* in so regarding it. A bottle that behaved like that *would* be a self. 'Handsome is that handsome does!' The bottle behaved like his mother, and therefore was like his mother. The point is, however, that he could not possibly come to this conclusion about the bottle unless he already possessed the idea of another self, which in this case was his mother. What is impossible to believe is that *any* peculiarity in an external body, even such a one as responsiveness, could suggest the presence of a second Ego to a mind which had hitherto worked with the picture of a world centred in a single Ego which was his own. Nor is it at all possible to believe that the baby first apprehends his mother as mere body and only afterwards as embodied spirit.

A view somewhat similar to Professor Stout's is defended by Professor Price in the article already referred to. It is, he holds, through the medium

All this is not to say that inference has no part to play in our knowledge of one another. Clearly it has a very large part to play. An inferential element is involved, first, in our *identification* of a particular self as a self—as when I have to decide during a visit to Madame Tussaud's whether the policeman in front of me is a wax figure or a living guardian of the law. An inferential element is involved, second, in the guidance afforded me towards my interpretation of the character of others by my observation of their bodily behaviour, and above all of their speech. What we are demanding, then, is not the exclusion of an inferential element but the inclusion of an element that is not inferential. And again there are two ways in which the presence of this latter must be recognized. First, it must be allowed that, whatever be true of subsequent encounters, the idea that other minds exist, or may exist, could not possibly have come to us in the first instance as the result of an inference. Rather is this idea itself the necessary presupposition of the only kind of inference that could be here in question. As

of *words* that we come to know other minds. With this I should cordially agree, for nothing could be more in line with the new teaching. But Professor Price goes on to explain that we first apprehend words as mere *noises* and then proceed to *deduce* their symbolic character by a process of analogical inference. 'It is the perceiving and understanding of noises and other symbols which gives one evidence for the existence of other minds.' 'At first it does not occur to one that the noises *are* symbols. One has to discover this for oneself. And one discovers it by learning to use them as symbols in one's own thinking.' Professor Price, however, goes on to admit that the process by which this happens is 'very puzzling, and I do not profess to have given anything like an adequate account of it.' It is here, as it seems to me, that his theory breaks down.

Cf. also J. Laird, *Problems of the Self*, p. 26.

Professor Hocking says, 'We are able to read our signs as we do, because we already expect them to mean something, we have already formed somehow the conception of another mind.'[1] Second, this non-inferential element which lies at the root of our social experience and was present at its birth, must also be allowed to be present throughout the whole subsequent course of it, playing at every point a necessary and constitutive part. It is thus, indeed, that the intuitive and the discursive elements in experience always intermingle. The discursive element is at every point present, at no point fundamental. It is essentially of the nature of a construction, grounded upon one intuition, and forming a bridge to another.

There is then an element of immediacy in our knowledge of one another. Our knowledge of other minds is not merely a derivative from our knowledge of other bodies or of our own minds or of both together, but is itself a primary and original mode of consciousness of equal right with these others and having, like them, a character *sui generis*. Expressing it in Kantian language, we may say that the conception of society is not an *a posteriori* but an *a priori* conception. It need hardly be said that this logical priority does not imply the chronological priority of the conception of society to actual social experience, still less anything that could be called its 'innateness'.[2] We cannot possess the conception of otherness prior to our first encounter with another, yet

[1] Op. cit., p. 250.
[2] It is a pity, I think, that Buber allows himself to speak of '*das einge-borene Du*' (op. cit., p. 35).

that conception is not inductively derived from the encounter, but is called into being on occasion of it and contributes to it the very character which would be required as the basis of such an induction; just as the conception of tridimensional space, though it could not be present in my mind prior to my first encounter with a solid body, is not derived by induction from that encounter, but is given with it as the necessary condition of its taking place—that is, as the necessary condition of my apprehending the body's solidity. The view that our knowledge of our neighbours depends on analogical projection is thus seen to be but a special case of the empiricist fallacy which Kant was so instrumental in exposing.

Furthermore, it must be allowed, or rather insisted upon, that the recognition of other minds, though it is not built up from the perception of the bodies associated with these minds but is itself an apprehension of a direct and primary kind, is nevertheless never given save in conjunction with such perception.[1] To suppose that I intuit the mental existence of my friends prior to my perception of their bodies is but the opposite error to that of supposing that I first apprehend my friends as mere bodily appearances and then infer their mentality from the behaviour of their bodies. To take either view would be to contravene our principle that no one of the

[1] Telepathy, even if proven, does not form an exception to this. In telepathy, we do not know other minds, but receive ideas from other minds without knowing these minds—even without knowing (except by inference) that it is from other minds that we receive them. This has been pointed out by Professor Price in the article already quoted.

four kinds of knowledge is ever given in abstraction from the other three. To take either view would be to import into primitive human consciousness the highly sophisticated dualism of soul and body, *res cogitans* and *res extensa*, which is now so familiar to ourselves as a legacy first from Greek and then from Cartesian philosophy. We are born, both as a race and as individuals, not into many worlds but into a single world; a world neither of dead bodies nor of shadowy ghosts, but a world at once living and solid. The 'animatist' outlook (if not the animist one exactly) is primitive both in the individual and in the race. We first recognize our fellow men neither as soulless bodies nor yet as discarnate souls but only as living, acting, and thinking beings—embodied souls or animated bodies.

I have compared our direct intuition of a world of other selves to our direct intuition of a tridimensional space. The comparison is, of course, borrowed from Dr. Heim, whose book is largely devoted to the development of it. Dr. Heim proposes the extension of this originally spatial conception of dimensionality to include all primary modes of apprehension; indeed he even proposes that the word space itself (*Raum*) should be given this extended usage. The intuition of a world of others, he holds, is strictly analogous to our intuition of a new spatial dimension in so far as it cannot be derived from any kind of consciousness that does not already contain it, but is rather the condition than the result of our recognition of certain particular beings as being in this way other than ourselves. There are indeed certain modifications of the bidimensional image printed on my retina which I learn to interpret as signs of tridimensionality in the external scene which that image reflects, just as there are tricks of painting on a flat canvas which at once create the impression of solidity in the object depicted. But in neither case would the impression of solidity be conveyed to a being who was not independently endowed with a tridimensional mode of apprehension. So also it is with our knowledge of our fellow men. We come to know their minds through the medium of words or other signs; these words or signs are noises or other events in the physical world; but their revelatory significance must for ever have been hidden from us, had we not been gifted with a social dimension of consciousness. 'The "Thou" relation shows with especial clearness that no knowledge of the reality in which we find ourselves placed is possible unless we presuppose, along with our observation of contents and the conclusions we may draw from such observation, a primary mode of knowledge in which we become aware of a structure of "spaces". No mere act of seeing can prove that my unbounded self yet has a boundary, that a frontier marks Me off from You, that your existence challenges all my pictures of the world. There is absolutely nothing of You that I can see. Telescope or microscope will not help. For my consciousness, You are transcendent. Nevertheless I have knowledge of You.'[1] 'The knowledge which the I has of the Thou, making it possible for the I to interpret a particular sound as a

[1] Heim, op. cit., English translation, p. 171.

"Word", comes about through a mode of knowledge which precedes observation of contents.'[1]

Our knowledge of other mind is therefore, like our knowledge of tridimensional space and all other primary modes of knowledge, something that cannot be imagined by one who does not already possess it, since it cannot be described to him in terms of anything else than itself. Nevertheless it may be very fully described in its own terms, and in such a way as to bring the essential characteristics of it very strikingly before those whose consciousness it already informs. It is to this description that writers like Dr. Buber and Dr. Grisebach have made so valuable a contribution. 'The tacit assumption', wrote the late Professor Bowman, 'that experience is all of the subject-object type has played havoc with much European philosophy.'[2] But now the difference between the type of experience in which we are confronted with an object and that in which we are confronted with another subject, has been made clearer to us than ever before. We have been shown with great vividness the contrast between that situation in which I am myself the single centre of my own world and that other situation in which I find myself confronted with what claims to be another centre of the same world—a being in the knowing of whom I myself am known. Dr. Gogarten and others have used this contrast to explain the distinction between the standpoints of science and history.[3] Its profound

[1] Ibid., p. 230.
[2] *Studies in the Philosophy of Religion*, vol. ii, p. 239.
[3] Cf. also Adrian Coates, *A Basis of Opinion* (1938), p. 28: 'The scientist is concerned with the world of objects, the historian with other subjects.'

ethical bearings have been most fully worked out by Dr. Grisebach, the familiar Kantian imperative now appearing in the more explicit form, 'Never reduce the I-Thou relationship to the I-It relationship'. 'Never treat another subject merely as an object'. 'Never try to deal with another centre as if he were merely part of your own circumference.' Fascinating as all this is, however, we must resist the temptation to linger over it any longer, since it is after all not for its own sake that we are at present interested to explore the problem of our knowledge of our fellow men.

§ 18

OUR present interest is only in the light which this deeper understanding of our knowledge of other subjects casts upon the nature of our knowledge of God. 'The mutual relation of persons', said Dr. Webb in Aberdeen in 1919, 'seems to be that which bears by far the closest resemblance to the relation of the personal Soul to the Supreme Reality which we call Religion';[1] and it was thus that he was incited to make the notable contribution to our understanding of the mutual relations of persons to which I have already acknowledged my debt. The fact is that by far the greater part of the researches whose results were summarized in the foregoing section is of definitely theological origin. It is in the course of the attempt to understand our relations with God that we have come to this better understanding of our relations with one another.

Theology has often been concerned to establish the 'objectivity' of God and has used that word as a virtual synonym for His reality. Yet there is in that usage a possibility of serious misunderstanding, and against this misunderstanding Kierkegaard has protested by emphasizing rather the *subjectivity* of God. 'God', he says, 'is infinite subjectivity.' It would be difficult to exaggerate the influence which this revision of outlook has had upon contemporary religious thought. Alike to Dr. Barth and

[1] *Divine Personality and Human Life*, p. 192. This lecture anticipates much of the teaching of Dr. Webb's later lecture to the British Academy.

Dr. Heim 'God is always subject'. And Bowman writes that to confound the relation of subject to subject with the relation of subject to object 'is to perpetuate one or other of the various fallacies that are at the bottom of every error in religious thinking and in the religious life'.[1]

The subjectivity of God is, however, so likely to be misunderstood as meaning that God is part of *our* subjectivity that it is probably wiser to vary the phrase and speak rather of the *subjecthood* of God. That God is always subject does not mean that there is not a secondary sense in which, in being known as subject, He may be said to be the *object* of our cognition. 'With regard to the term "object of thought",' writes Mr. Adrian Coates, 'let us recognize that the word "object" is or may be used here in a secondary or metaphorical sense within the concept of perceptual existence.'[2] But what must at all costs be emphasized is that from the beginning God meets us, not as one among the many objects of our knowledge, but as another Knower by whom both they and we ourselves are known. He is not part of the world we know—there is nothing that is more deprecated by the Barthian theologians than the tendency to make God *ein Stück Welt*—rather is He another Knowledge of that world. He confronts us not as an It nor as an inference from all possible Its, but, from the very beginning, as a Thou. He is not something we find ourselves speaking *about*, but Some One we find speaking to us and whom we then, in our turn, find ourselves speaking *to*. He con-

[1] Op. cit., vol. ii, p. 319.   [2] *A Basis of Opinion*, p. 248.

fronts us in such a way that we know we must not speak about Him in the third person, but can only speak to Him in the second person. 'Properly speaking,' writes Dr. Buber, 'God cannot be expressed but only addressed.'[1] Up to a certain point the same is true of our relations with our fellow men. They also confront us from the beginning, not as mere objects known by us, nor yet as hypothetical existences deduced from the behaviour of the objects we know as their bodies, but as other subjects in the knowing of whom we know that we ourselves are known. And to them also, when they are present, the second-personal mode of speech is alone truly appropriate. We cannot speak *about* other people in their presence. The difference is, however, that our fellow men are not always present, nor always addressing us, whereas God is the Omnipresent Other, the Eternal Thou, by whom we are at every moment being addressed. God, says Dr. Buber, is 'the Thou which by its very nature cannot become It'.[2] And again, 'Only one Thou is in its very nature incapable of ceasing to be Thou for us. He who knows God knows well what is meant by being far from God . . . but the absence of God he does not know. It is only we who are not always there.'[3] Whereas, therefore, it may often be appropriate to speak

---

[1] '*angesprochen, nicht ausgesagt*'—op. cit., p. 95. The whole passage reads thus: 'It is not as if God could be inferred from anything—for instance, from nature as its Author, from history as its Controller, or from the subject as the Self which thinks itself in it. It is not as if something else were "given" and this afterwards deduced from it; rather is this the Being by which we are immediately, primarily and continuously confronted; who, properly speaking, cannot be expressed but only addressed.'

[2] Op. cit., p. 89.   [3] Ibid., p. 115.

of our fellows in the third person as 'He' or 'She'—though even here we must be on our guard against betrayal, when we speak, as it were behind their backs, of those who are not present—there is never a time when this third-personal language is fully appropriate to our relations with God—for God's back is never turned to us and we must never turn our backs to Him. Again, just because God is the omnipresent Knower, His knowledge of us precedes all our knowledge of Him, and His address to us precedes and conditions our address to Him, which is therefore always in the nature of a response. In the last resort it is always He who calls and we who answer. Whereas, in a meeting with a fellow man, it may happen that I am the first to be there and the first to speak. And once more, and again because He is omnipresent, there is nothing in our experience which may not be the medium of God's self-revelation; whereas our fellow men cannot address us save through the very limited and particular medium of their own bodily organization. In every relationship in which we stand, whether towards nature or towards men or towards the realm of essences, says Dr. Buber, 'we are regarding the hem of the garment of the eternal Thou; from each there reaches us a waft of His breath; in each Thou we address the eternal Thou'.[1]

It is, then, not as an object that may be spoken about, but as a Subject who must be spoken to, that God meets us. Shall we say 'meets us in our *experience*'? Dr. Buber would not allow such a phrase. He understands the word experience (the German *Erfahrung*) to designate the rela-

[1] Op. cit., p. 118.

tion between subject and object, and will not admit it as descriptive of the relation between subject and subject. I do not experience my friends, as I experience the external world; rather am I *in relation with* them. 'I do not experience the man to whom I say "Thou". But I stand in relation to him. . . . Only when I transgress the relation do I again experience him. Experience means the remoteness of the Thou.'[1] I may experience abstracted aspects of my friend, but in so abstracting these aspects as to make them objects of experience, I move out of my essential relation to him and he thereby ceases to be a Thou for me. 'I can take out from him the colour of his hair or the colour of his speech or the colour of his kindliness—indeed I must be doing this all the time; but when I do it, he is no longer a Thou.'[2] And so it must also be with reference to God. We know Him, but with the knowledge only of relation, not of experience. We stand in personal relation to Him but we must not say that we have experience of Him. To understand the strength of Dr. Buber's insistence on this point, we must notice that in his mind experiencing is very closely associated with 'making use of' or 'turning to account'. We use what we experience; we enjoy that with which (or rather those with whom) we stand in relation. Hence, because all the saints and theologians agree that we must not *uti deo* but only *frui deo*, it seems clear to Dr. Buber that we must not speak of experiencing God. 'The development of the power to experience and to use', he writes, 'comes about for the most part through the

[1] Ibid., p. 16.   [2] Ibid., p. 15.

weakening of man's power of relation—the power in respect of which alone man can live in the spirit.'[1] We cannot but connect this with much that has been said by the Barthian theologians against the conception of 'religious experience'. Yet perhaps the point is hardly more than a verbal one. I should myself have said that when Professor Farmer called one of his books *Experience of God*, the view he was defending was far from contradicting—was indeed rather strikingly similar to—Dr. Buber's conception of personal relation with God. The same is true of Bowman when he writes that 'we cannot be the subject of any experience without experiencing something of God'.[2] It may be that experience of God is not a very natural phrase and had best be avoided; but, if we do avoid it, we must remember that in Dr. Buber's view experience of men is a phrase no less to be avoided. And we must remember also that what takes the place of such experience is something not less but more direct and face-to-face, namely personal encounter.

It has been said that there is no moment of my life in which God does not approach me in a personal way, offering me some blessedness and making some demand upon my obedience. There is therefore no moment in which I can speak about God in a third-personal way, whether to myself or to you, without in some measure losing hold of the reality of the situation in which I stand. This is exactly the point of emergence of Kierkegaard's conception of existential thinking, to which reference has

[1] Op. cit., p. 49.
[2] Op. cit., vol. ii, p. 393: 'God's Personality as Experienced by Us.'

already been made as having, after long neglect, exercised a remarkable influence upon the theology of the post-War generation. As soon as God becomes merely the object of my thought, my thinking ceases to be thus existential. And yet, if theology is to proceed at all, if even the preaching of the word is to proceed, I *must* make God the object of my objective contemplation, speaking of Him, as I am doing now, in the third person. That, then, says Kierkegaard, is why theology can never be anything else but 'dialectical'. When we forsake the mode of address, which is the mode of prayer, our thought breaks up into dialectic, that is, is refracted in two contrary directions, so that no one statement we make about God can then be quite true unless it be supplemented and corrected by what, from this detached and third-personal point of view, appears to be its opposite. I have already[1] pointed out the close relation of this teaching, which is now most familiar to us in the form in which it appeared in Dr. Barth's early writings, to the Kantian doctrine that the 'practical' knowledge of God given us in our direct dealings with Him cannot be validly used for the extension of our 'theoretical' knowledge of a supersensible world. 'The last source of dialectics', writes Dr. Theodor Haecker in his fine essay on Kierkegaard, 'is the person in so far as it has to be thought, that is to say, in so far as the person becomes the object, is objectivized; for in the widest sense everything which has to be thought must be objectivized. But the person, subjectivity, cannot become the object, yet must, if it is

[1] See above, § 14 *ad fin.*

to be known; so that, by the very fact of thinking it, something essential is taken from it, subjectivity, and something added to it which fundamentally it is not, objectivity. With such a point in view how could Kierkegaard not be a dialectician?'[1]

It is clear, then, that our knowledge of God is no less travestied than is our knowledge of one another, when it is regarded as being merely inferential in nature. To Kierkegaard, says Dr. Haecker, 'it seemed absurd and insulting to set about proving the existence of an ever-present person'.[2] 'We can no more *prove* God's existence', writes Professor de Burgh, 'than we can *prove* that of our fellow men; our knowledge of the one as of the other is founded on the experience of their presence.'[3] It is here that so much of the best thought of our time is in revolt against the intellectualism which is as characteristic of medieval scholasticism as of the *saeculum rationalisticum* itself—the intellectualism which makes over too large a field of human experience to the discursive as distinct from the perceptive (or intuitive) reason—the νοῦς αἰσθητικός, as it was called by the Greeks. To those with whom God has had any personal dealings at all, atheism should be as artificial an academic hypothesis as is the hypothesis of solipsism to those who have had any dealings with their fellow men; while to those, if such existed, with whom God has had no such

---

[1] *Sören Kierkegaard*, by Theodor Haecker, translated by Alexander Dru (1937), p. 31.　　　　[2] Ibid., p. 47.

[3] *Towards a Religious Philosophy*, p. 169. Dr. Buber, as we have seen, would boggle at Professor de Burgh's use of the word experience in this connexion.

dealings, argument would be as little use as it would be to those, if *they* existed, who had never met a fellow man. I know of no statement of the matter that seems to me more exactly right-minded than that of Sir Arthur Eddington in his Swarthmore Lecture on *Science and the Unseen World*: 'In the case of our human friends we take their existence for granted, not caring whether it is proven or not. Our relationship is such that we could read philosophical arguments designed to prove the non-existence of each other, and perhaps even be convinced by them—and then laugh together over so odd a conclusion. I think that it is something of the same kind of security we should seek in our relationship with God. The most flawless proof of the existence of God is no substitute for it; and if we have that relationship the most convincing disproof is turned harmlessly aside. If I may say it with reverence, the soul and God laugh together over so odd a conclusion.'[1]

[1] Op. cit., p. 43.

§ 19

'GOD is either not there at all', writes Dr. Heim, 'or else He is the single ineluctable Thou before whom all creatures continually stand. So when I am with Him, I am with all my fellow creatures.'[1] He is, as we have said, the absolute and omnipresent Other in which all others have their ground. But the question may now be raised whether One who is thus absolute and omnipresent can be regarded merely as Another who stands over against me. In human intra-personal intercourse you and I do stand merely over against one another; you are wholly other than I, however closely we may be related. But if God is the absolute ground of my being, then it may be doubted whether He can be said to be wholly other than I.

Dr. Barth, Dr. Brunner, and Dr. Heim, who in so many other respects are opposed to one another, have all followed Rudolf Otto in teaching that 'God is wholly other'. Yet the discussion that has raged round this dictum has at all times been clouded in confusion. Wholly other may mean two quite different things according as it is understood with reference to numerical identity or to qualitative resemblance. One pea may be so *like* another pea as to be indistinguishable from it—in accordance with the common saying, 'as like as two peas'—and yet they are entirely different peas. There is therefore one sense in which the second pea is *not at*

[1] *Glaube und Denken* (1931), p. 316 f.

228

all other than the first, and another sense in which it is *wholly* other than it. Now, when God is spoken of by these contemporary theologians as being wholly other than man, part of the meaning almost always seems to be that He is wholly unlike man. But, since it is ground common to all theologians that man was *originally* made in God's image and likeness, his alleged present total unlikeness to God can be due only to the total destruction of the original likeness through sin and the Fall. It is in this sense that Principal Cairns understands the current use of the phrase 'wholly other' when he repudiates it as 'clean against the teaching of Scripture'.[1] And against such a doctrine of the *total* corruption of human nature I have already given my own very emphatic verdict. But even if this be granted, God may still be wholly other than I in the sense of numerical identity. Though not wholly unlike me, He may yet be wholly distinct from me, wholly over against me, confronting me wholly from without myself. It is this 'over-againstness' of God, as von Hügel used to call it, that we have been so much concerned to emphasize, but now we must raise the question whether this conception is in itself large enough to embrace the whole truth.

We cannot doubt that religion is essentially a relationship between two distinct subjects, a 'traffic of Jacob's ladder' between God and man. There was therefore every need for our being recalled from the vagaries and excesses of nineteenth-century immanentism to a proper realization of the transcendence of God, and of what the

[1] *The Riddle of the World* (1937), p. 325.

Westminster Confession calls the 'so great . . . distance between God and the creature'.[1] The question is whether the situation can be righted only by taking refuge in the opposite extreme and denying that there is any truth whatever in the thought of divine immanence. Is the relation between God and the soul of man to be understood as an external relation merely? Is God in no sense *in* the soul, but only presents Himself *to* the soul; just as you, my fellow man, are not in me but only present yourself to me? The mistake of immanentism was that it lost hold of the vital distinction between Creator and creature, and to-day we are all most anxious to restore that distinction. But, in our praiseworthy anxiety to restore it, are we to press it home to the extent of saying that the soul of man, no less than the stocks and stones, is a *mere* creature, a *merely* 'made' thing—the work of God's hands but having no participation in God's being?

The orthodox Christian teaching is that God created all things out of nothing; the body of man He made from the soil of the earth which in its turn He had created out of nothing; the soul of man He created out of nothing and joined it to the body 'in a wonderful union of substance'.[2] But it is also part of the orthodox teaching that God, in creating man out of nothing, created him in His own image and likeness, so that 'in a very special way man imitates the nature of God'.[3] He *imitates* God's nature, but St. Thomas Aquinas will not allow that in

[1] VII. i.
[2] Gasparri, *The Catholic Catechism*, English translation, p. 78.
[3] Ibid.

any sense he *participates in* God's nature. Though like God, he is wholly distinct from God. In no sense does the soul partake of the substance of God.[1] There is therefore no divinity in the soul of man, nor is the soul in any sense made divine by the infusion into it of divine grace. There is no *participatio divinitatis*. It is well known that many earlier Christian thinkers had spoken of a divine element in the soul, and of the salvation of the soul as its deification, but against all such tendencies St. Thomas resolutely sets his face. This stout stand of his must, however, be understood in relation to his strong anti-mystical tendency which made him deny to man all vision of the essence or substance of God. It is just because man does not participate in the essence of God that he cannot even in the least degree attain to a vision of it; and if after death the blessed are granted a partial vision (which still falls short of a full comprehension),[2] that can only be by some supernatural 'influx of divine light' which transforms the nature of the soul. Calvin occupies exactly the same ground. He argues hotly against the doctrine that the verse in Genesis which says that God breathed into man's nostrils the breath of life is to be taken as meaning 'that the soul was a transmission of the substance of God, as if some portion of the boundless divinity had passed into man'.[3] It is not God, but only a resemblance to God, that is in man—or rather that was in him originally and may be restored through Christ. It is this resemblance

---

[1] *Summa contra Gentiles*, ii. 85: 'That the Soul is not of the Substance of God.'

[2] Ibid. lv.   [3] *Institutio*, I. xv, § 5.

which is constitutive of human nature, extending as it does to 'everything in which the nature of man surpasses that of all other animal species'.[1]

The question set for us afresh by modern immanent-ism is whether this conception of resemblance without participation can really be carried out. Vital as is the distinction between uncreated and created reality, and tragic as have been the results of our recent forgetfulness of it, is it possible that it was elevated by medievalism into too complete a dualism? That 'it belongs to God alone to create',[2] and that man has no share in God's creativity, is to St. Thomas a fundamental principle. Modern philosophy, on the contrary, has found creativity everywhere—in all living things and above all in the operations of man's mind. That such philosophy has gone wildly astray we cannot doubt. But are we to believe that there is no glimpse of truth in it at all? Are we to believe that life and mind are purely 'made' things? Or should we not rather say that man has creativity, though a creativity of a delegated and derivative kind? The difficulty is to see how without creativity there can be any freedom. The two concepts seem to run into one another, if indeed they are not one and the same concept. It would seem that a delegated freedom, such as we must believe man to possess, implies also some sort of dele-gated creativeness. If we are regarded merely as the work of God's hands, as are the *trunci et lapides* of the natural world, then it is difficult to see how we can be any more responsible for the origination of our actions than they

---

[1] Calvin, op. cit., I. xv, § 3.   [2] *Summa contra Gentiles*, ii. 21.

are for theirs.[1] It may be questioned whether the denial to man of all participation in the divine nature, and of even a delegated creativity, does not tend to issue in a denial of all liberty in human action. Calvin does not deny such liberty, but it may perhaps be said that he has some difficulty in finding a place for it within his scheme. Nor does St. Thomas escape from all difficulty. He believes man to be a free agent, and defines such a free agent as one who is *causa sui* or *sibi causa agendi*, who is 'master of his own actions';[2] yet how are we to separate self-causation from true origination, and true origination from creativity? Here is a problem which the religious philosophy of our time is urgently called upon to face.

My own chief doubt concerning the total repudiation of immanence and participation arises, however, from another set of considerations—though they are considerations that still concern the question of freedom. The reason why it is difficult to regard the relation of

---

[1] In the most recent (and a most clarifying) treatment of the free will problem, namely, Professor C. Arthur Campbell's Inaugural Address on his appointment to the Chair of Logic in Glasgow, free will seems to be identified with creativeness *tout court*. See *In Defence of Free Will* (Glasgow, 1938). Cf. Kemp Smith, *Is Divine Existence Credible?*, p. 11. 'The self is, indeed, like all other existences, capable of creativity; but it is a conditioned and delegated creativity; and if we are to believe in a Divine Being on analogy of the self, we must carry over into the conception of it all that is thus mysterious in the self, at the same time recognizing its possession of a creativity which is not thus conditioned and creaturely, and which is therefore proportionately the more mysterious.' For a defence of the view that God 'creates creators', see W. R. Matthews, *Studies in Christian Philosophy* (1921), pp. 206 ff.

[2] *Summa contra Gentiles*, i. 88, § 4; ii. 48, § 2.

man to God as merely a relationship between two beings who stand over against each other (and are in that sense wholly other) is that *God appears in some sort to be present on both sides of the relationship.*[1] When I respond to God's call, the call is God's and the response is mine; and yet the response is God's too; for not only does He call me in His grace, but also by His grace brings the response to birth within my soul. His Holy Spirit is the real author and originator, not only of His address to me, but of my address to Him. For is He not the sole author of *all* good? As the hymn says:

> All, save the clouds of sin, are Thine.[2]

or again:

> And every virtue we possess,
> And every victory won,
> And every thought of holiness
> Are His alone.[3]

And who is it that has said that 'the only thing of my very own which I contribute to my salvation is the sin from which I need to be redeemed'? And yet though all that is in us of good or of responsiveness is His, and in the last resort even His *alone*, yet it is truly our own *as well*. Indeed there is nothing that is more truly our own. We are never more truly ourselves than when we do nothing but what is done by the Spirit of God in us. The

[1] Cf. W. G. de Burgh, *From Morality to Religion* (1938), p. 259: 'Our answering love is the very spirit of God working within us. God is present, so to speak, on both sides in the reciprocal relation.'

[2] Oliver Wendell Holmes, 'Lord of all being'.

[3] Harriet Auber, 'Our blest Redeemer'.

same deed may therefore be my deed in the fullest and truest sense, and yet be purely God's deed within me. 'I live,' says St. Paul, 'yet not I, but Christ liveth in me.'[1] Such is the mysterious relationship between divine grace and human freedom.[2] And again I must say, not only of any little good I have been enabled to do, but of the much greater good that has been done to me, that it is all of God. And yet nearly all this good—nearly all the blessings of which I have been the unworthy recipient—have come to me through the free will of my fellow men, through my mother's self-sacrifice for my sake, through the kindness and generosity of a host of men and women, some teachers, some lifelong friends, some casual acquaintances and 'ships that pass in the night'. I thank them all, but I thank God too. For the same deed I thank them both; and not for different parts or shares of it, as say the Synergists and Molinists with their talk of a *concursus simultaneus*; but I thank God for the whole of it, and under God I thank them for the whole of it too. Moreover, what is true of grace is true of inspiration. In the Bible it is God who speaks to us, yet every word we read in it was also spoken—and thought and written— by man. 'It is not', so runs a famous saying of Dr. Barth's, 'the right human thoughts about God which form the

---

[1] Galatians ii. 20.

[2] To be surrendered, says von Hügel, is to 'allow God to make you do yourself actively not that which He desires you to submit to, but that which He desires you to do. We are acted upon only in that measure in which we ourselves act. *Non est deus mortuorum'*—quoted from *The Mystical Element of Religion* by Maurice Nédoncelle, *La Pensée religieuse de Friedrich von Hügel*, English translation, p. 162.

content of the Bible, but the right divine thoughts about men.'[1] And yet every one of these right divine thoughts about men was thought out also by one or other of the Biblical authors. When God speaks to us in the Epistle, it is at the same time St. Paul who speaks to us. St. Paul's thinking is not extinguished, but is rather at its best, when God is most plainly thinking in Him. And again, when Christ promised His disciples that in the hour when they should be haled before kings and councils it should be given them what they should speak, 'for it is not ye that speak, but the Holy Ghost',[2] He did not mean that they would be expressing, as it were automatically, something other than their own thought.

These or similar reflections will be again before us in our next and concluding section, and need not be further dwelt upon now. It will hardly be denied that they touch the very core of the Christian faith. Yet it is difficult to find expression for them within the terms of a purely transitive relation between God and man, conceived as wholly distinct in being. Dr. Buber so fears the dissolution of such relatedness into any kind of identity that he baulks even at the saying 'I and my Father are one', and appears to hold, in opposition to the Christian tradition, that the Father and the Son are merely 'like' in substance (*Wesensgleich*), and in no sense one in being.[3] Properly understood, he insists, the Gospel of John, though it has often been read in a mystical sense,

---

[1] *The Word of God and the Word of Man* (English translation of *Das Wort Gottes und die Theologie*), p. 43.

[2] Mark xiii. 11.

[3] Op. cit., p. 100. Dr. Buber, though he thus argues, is himself a Jew.

is 'the Gospel of pure relatedness'. But our query is whether, when the Thou becomes absolute, our relation to it can any longer be exhaustively understood as a relation of I to Thou. For the Absolute must be behind the response of the I in a way which is impossible for one who merely stands over against the I as a Thou. There is a point beyond which our relation to one another ceases to be analogous to our relation to God. How can God be only over against me, if all the good I do is wholly His and yet most truly done by me, if all the truth I think is wholly His and yet most truly thought by me, and if I am never so truly myself as when He does in me what He wills and thinks in me what He would have me think? How can He be wholly other than I, if I am most truly *causa mei* when I am being most irresistibly determined by Him?

It would seem then that, great as is the service which Dr. Barth has rendered us in weaning us from the entice-ments of a one-sided immanentism, he has tended to lead us astray in his apparent complete rejection of the truth for which immanentism and mysticism alike contend.[1] And probably when the theological excitement of these present years gives place to a period of calmer reflection, it will be recognized that von Hügel was here the safer

---

[1] Dr. Barth, attempting to do justice to the New Testament language about the indwelling of the Spirit, does indeed in one or two places speak of God as being not only transcendent but immanent. But he interprets this immanence as *presence to*, and not as *presence in*. 'In standing over against the World that He has made', he writes, 'God is present to it—not only far, but also near. . . . We are concerned with the transcendence of God the Creator. The knowledge of that compels the recognition of His immanence also.'—*Credo*, English translation, p. 34.

guide. It is wiser with the latter to recognize 'the mystical element' in Christianity alongside of other and even more dominating elements than with the former to treat mysticism as a mere *alternative* to Christianity. 'For', writes von Hügel, 'it is evident that, between affirming the simple Divinity of the innermost centre of the soul, and declaring that the soul ever experiences only the Grace of God, i.e. certain created effects, sent by Him from the far-away seat of His own full presence, there is room for a middle position which, whilst ever holding the definite creatureliness of the soul, in all its reaches, puts God Himself into the soul and the soul into God, in degrees and with results which vary indeed indefinitely according to its goodwill and its call, yet which all involve and constitute a presence ever profoundly real, ever operative before and beyond all the soul's own operations.'[1] If anything like this is true, then the indwelling of the Holy Spirit of God in the heart of man is a togetherness of a more complex and intimate kind than any relation that can exist between one finite spirit and another. The relation between two individual personalities cannot be entirely analogous to that between one individual personality and

[1] *The Mystical Element of Religion*, 2nd edition, vol. ii, p. 336. On the same page von Hügel writes: 'Only the soul's ineradicable capacity, need and desire for its Divine Lodger and Sustainer would constitute, in this conception, the intrinsic characteristic of human nature; and it is rather the too close identification, in feeling and emotional expression, of the desire and the Desired, of the hunger and the Food, and the too exclusive realization of the deep truth that this desire and hunger do not cause, but are themselves preceded and caused by, their Object—it is the over-vivid perception of this real dynamism, rather than any *a priori* theory of static substances and identities—which certainly, in many cases, has produced the appearance of Pantheism.'

Another who is not only individual personality but also Personality Itself. The relation of two good men to each other must be less close than the relation of a good man to One who is not only good but Goodness, and not only loving but Love. Distant though God be in His transcendence, He may yet be nearer to me than my best friend. And then to say that I am *addressed* by God from without myself, though it expresses—as we have been at so great pains to insist—a vital truth, does not express the only truth. Nor can we believe that there is no other way of conceiving the approach of God to man than as the speaking of a *Word* which man is called upon to hear. To do justice to the richness of that relationship many other conceptions are needed also; as in 'The Breastplate of St. Patrick':

> Christ be with me, Christ within me,
> Christ behind me, Christ before me,
> Christ beside me, Christ to win me,
> Christ to comfort and restore me,
> Christ beneath me, Christ above me,
> Christ in quiet, Christ in danger,
> Christ in hearts of all that love me,
> Christ in mouth of friend and stranger.

§ 20

'THE duty of the clergyman', says Ruskin in *Unto This Last*, 'is to remind people in an eloquent manner of the existence of God.' Such a remark makes it clear that argument, in spite of all we have said against a certain use of it, has a true office to perform with respect to the divine existence, just as we saw it to have with respect to the existence of our fellow men. For though we may not try to prove either to ourselves or to others that God exists, we may do something to persuade both ourselves and others *that we already believe in Him*; just as it is true that though we cannot prove to the solipsist that his fellow men exist, we can do something to prove to him that he already believes in their existence. Such is the only legitimate kind of theistic proof. 'The true business of philosophy', wrote Cook Wilson in words which I have already quoted, 'seems to be to bring the belief to a consciousness of itself.'[1] It is to this end that the whole argument of this book has been directed, and I must try now to bring the matter to a head.

The argument has never been better expressed than in the familiar words of Pascal. Never was there a more troubled seeker after God than Pascal, but his comfort came to him when he heard God say, 'Thou wouldst not be seeking me, hadst thou not already found me. Be not therefore disquieted.'[2] All we can say will be an expansion of that.

[1] Op. cit., vol. ii, p. 851.
[2] *Pensées*, ed. Brunschvicg, 555. But Browning's Bishop Blougram

Of recent years the tendency has been to start from the feeling of reverence or awe of which all men are conscious as being called forth by their experience of reality, and to argue that this betokens their recognition in that reality of something which is *holy*. This is the route which was followed by Windelband in his essay on *Das Heilige*[1] (which I first read in Cologne just after the Armistice in a *Feldpostausgabe*—a penny edition which had been printed for the use of the German troops), by Cook Wilson in the paper to which I have so often alluded, and by Rudolf Otto in the widely read book to which he gave the same title as Windelband had given to his essay. It is in itself an excellent route, yet I am convinced that in trying to follow it out Otto and those whom he has influenced have gone seriously astray. Since I have already offered so full a criticism of Otto's construction in another place,[2] and since it has been dealt with along similar lines by many other writers, I shall do no more here than indicate the main result. Otto's view seems to be that the determinative element in the religious sentiment of reverence or awe is what might be called the feeling of *eeriness*. This he believes to be a feeling of an entirely unique and uncompounded kind, and to testify to the presence in the reality which calls it forth of an element of *Schauerlichkeit* or 'shuddersomeness', or even of 'spookiness'—for Otto appeals in explanation of his meaning to the German phrase '*Es spukt hier!*' And goes too far in his paraphrase: 'If you desire faith, then you've faith enough.'

[1] Originally printed in his *Präludien*.
[2] *The Interpretation of Religion*, pp. 246–55.

he feels that it is to the persistence of this underivable and 'unevolvable' (*unentwickelbar*) feeling that religion owes its characteristic quality. The higher manifestations of religion differ from the lower neither in respect of the disappearance of this element nor in respect of its further development, but only in respect of its increasing association with something that Otto denies to be in itself characteristically religious at all, namely, morality. Such is perhaps as accurate an account of this doctrine as can be compressed into so short a compass. The fundamental heresy of it lies in its dissociation of the ultimate springs of our moral consciousness from all that is religious. Such a dissociation seems to me to be as fatal to a true understanding of the essence of morality as of the essence of religion. For while, on the one hand, morality loses its essential character if we take away from it that truly 'numinous' attitude of reverence which (in his doctrine of *Achtung*) it was the great merit of Kant to describe as its only true core, no less does religion, on the other hand, lose its essential character if it be reduced to a mere sense of eeriness in the presence of a mysterious something which may not yet have come to be regarded as having any rightful or righteous claim upon our obedience. It seems to me that we know enough from our own experience of the true nature of religion to justify our denial of the name of it to all ghostly shudders that bear no birth-relationship to the solemn claims of righteousness. 'That sort of thing may *look* like religion', we say, 'but it is not the genuine article; it has not the root of the matter in it at all.' And if indeed (which is exceedingly doubtful) there are any savage tribes who, though conscious of no rightful claim that their gods make upon their lives and no benefit they can receive from them, nevertheless bow down before them in worship, then we must believe that this represents the vestige of some true religious feeling which has now been lost rather than the seed which was afterwards to grow into the faith of the saints.

Whatever opinions we may hold 'with the top or our minds' about the existence of God, there is *something* which every one of us recognizes as holy, and before this holy thing we are all ready to bow in reverence. But I believe we are all well able to distinguish this, which is the true holy, from the spurious eeriness associated with ghostly superstitions. We do not really feel *reverence* in the supposed presence of a ghost. That which is truly holy to us all, and which calls forth reverence in us, is always some loyalty, some standard, some principle, some ideal—it may be only of sportsmanship or the honour of 'the old school tie', or of gentlemanliness or chivalry, or again of things like business honesty or scientific disinterestedness, but it may also be of some deeper and finer quality of saintliness. In other words, where we meet the holy thing is always in some holy *demand* that is made upon our lives. What is holy to us somehow resides in what we know we ought to be. Something is being asked of us, expected of us, and it is at the source of that expectation that the holiness lies. Yet not all demands that are made upon us are thus associated with the sentiment of reverence, but only those demands whose right is recognized by us as being *unconditional* or *absolute*—those demands which Kant distinguished from merely hypothetical imperatives as being *categorical*. If a man ask himself 'What things must I rather die than betray?' then he will know what things for him are holy. And Kant was fully justified in his contention that in presence of such unconditional demands we are aware in ourselves of a sentiment of a wholly unique kind, different from all earthly desires, and to which he gave the not very adequate name of *respect*. Now there is no doubt that in the consciousness of mankind as a whole, before it has been disturbed by the latter-day representations of philosophic atheism, this final demand that is made upon our wills is directly apprehended by us as a claim made upon us by a holy and personal Being to whom we give the name of God. The only argument with which we can properly meet those atheistic representations is therefore one which consists in the demonstration that the recognition of such an unconditional obligation does in fact contain in itself the recognition of a holy God who is its source. This argument would, as I conceive it, consist in the defence of two propositions; first, that *no obligation can be absolute which does not derive from the Absolute* (or unconditional which does not derive from the Unconditioned)—a truth that becomes all the more luminous if we adopt Kierkegaard's version of the Kantian imperative, 'Relate thyself absolutely to the Absolute and relatively to the relative'; and second, that, since morality is essentially a function of personality, we can feel no moral obligation to an Absolute who is not apprehended by us as a personal being—or, as Professor Farmer has recently expressed it, 'The awareness of God as personal will is given immediately in the impact of unconditional value itself.'[1] I shall not now repeat what I have said elsewhere in support of these propositions,[2] but I have every confidence that they will increasingly commend themselves to careful thinking.

Our argument must, however, proceed a stage further. For it is of no less importance to recognize clearly that this absolute demand is not felt by us as the mere imposition of alien authority. If it were so alien, it could not appear to us as holy nor could we reverence it as we do. The reverence we pay to it is called forth by the clear knowledge that only in yielding to it can we find *our own* highest good. This obedience is indeed laid upon us by that which is other than ourselves, yet we know that only in yielding to this Other can our own true selfhood be realized. The question which the doubter must here ask himself is, therefore, whether there be not an absolute obedience in which alone he can find fullest self-expression, *whether there be not a complete surrender in which alone he can find perfect liberty.* It is here we touch upon the most mysterious paradox, which is also the most critically significant fact, of the spiritual life—that deeper-lying

---

[1] *The World and God* (1935), p. 24. Cf. also Bowman, op. cit., vol. ii: 'Obligation is a corollary of the contractual element in personal relations' (p. 101). 'Man's obligations to his fellow men are either a fiction, an artifact of his own devising, or else they are the articulations of a single all-inclusive obligation which he owes to God' (p. 104).

[2] In my *Interpretation of Religion*, pp. 346–56, 389–92. But in the context of these passages there is much that I would not now express as I expressed it then.

paradox which lies behind the much-noticed paradox of hedonism that 'to get pleasure you must forget it'. Kant was wide awake to its importance when he framed his doctrine of the autonomy of the moral will which 'is not subject simply to the law, but so subject that it must be regarded as itself giving the law';[1] but the true depth of it was nevertheless hidden from him. The autonomy of the self-legislating will is only one side of the familiar truth; the other side of it is that only within a final heteronomy can such autonomy be realized. Taken by itself, the idea of obedience to a law of which our own wills are the source is a self-destructive and nonsensical idea; for the man who is a law unto himself does not live by law at all. Sense can be made of it only if we go on to say that the will which we are thus called upon to obey is indeed another Will than ours, yet a Will in obedience to which we can alone find our own true selfhood and our wills their real freedom. In attempting to do justice to the dignity of man as personal spirit the Kantian doctrine of autonomy thus forgets the creatureliness of his personality; it forgets what Tennyson so well remembered when he wrote, 'Our wills are ours, to make them Thine'.[2] Man is indeed an 'end in himself', but only after he has first found his selfhood in an end beyond himself —which is the glory of God.

J'ai fui partout; partout j'ai retrouvé la Loi,
  Quelque chose en moi qui soit plus moi-même que moi.[3]

[1] *Grundlegung zur Metaph. d. Sitten, Zweiter Abschnitt.*
[2] *In Memoriam, ad init.*   [3] Paul Claudel, *Vers d'Exil.*

There is, then, a self-surrender in which our true selves are handed back to us. There is an obedience which brings to the soul such a sense of release as it can never find when itself is its only law. There is Another Will whose service is perfect freedom. *In la sua volontade è nostra pace.*[1] Whoever is aware of this is aware of God, even if he is not aware that he is aware of Him. For such a one has been confronted with a Presence to whom he must now say:

> My will is not my own
> Till Thou hast made it Thine;
> If it would reach a monarch's throne
> It must its crown resign;
> It only stands unbent
> Amid the clashing strife,
> When on Thy bosom it has leant
> And found in Thee its life.[2]

In this way we know also that the authority we here encounter is that of One who loves us better than we love ourselves. He with whom we have in the last resort to reckon is not only our sovereign Overlord but also our Refuge and our Strength. If the obedience He demands of us is with a sole view to His own glory, it is also with a view to our salvation; and that is not a contradiction, because it is only in the glory of God that we can ever find salvation. This is where every merely moralistic system of thought falls short of the wholeness of even the most elemental spiritual experience. No submission,

[1] Dante, *Paradiso*, Canto III.
[2] George Matheson, 'Make me a captive, Lord, And then I shall be free.'

however humble, is of the nature of true religion unless it be a *trusting* submission, unless its Law be also a Gospel, unless its humility be the humble acceptance of a gracious salvation already accomplished by God Himself. In our very earliest awareness of the encompassing Will of God are already contained the seeds of the knowledge that His banner over us is love.

And this recognition of love brings with it the sentiment of gratitude. The dominating part which this sentiment plays in the religious consciousness has seldom had justice done to it in the philosophy of religion, yet there are few facts to which the religious literatures of the world bear more striking testimony. The Bible is a veritable library of God's praise. And there is no text in the New Testament that better sums up the whole message of it than the saying of St. Paul, 'Thanks be unto God for his unspeakable gift.'[1] Here again, as it seems to me, the general consciousness of mankind contains the germ of a religious response to the encompassing reality. For I believe that even those who think they do not believe in God do nevertheless in some degree possess the knowledge, not only that something is being demanded of them, and that this demand is fundamentally a demand that they should accept something that is being offered them, but also that here is something for which it behoves them to be *thankful*. To go through life with a heart full of praise—men do somehow know that that is the most admirable way to live. Writing in one of her letters of her delight in a lovely spot in the Alps, Katherine

[1] 2 Corinthians ix. 15.

Mansfield exclaims, 'If only one could make some small grasshoppery sound of praise to some one, thanks to some one—but who?' There were the impulse to gratitude and the intuitive knowledge of the appropriateness of gratitude, surviving even the long-established reign of the intellectual doubt as to whether there existed a Being who could properly be the object of such gratitude. Yet it is clear that the sentiment of gratitude implicitly contains in itself the recognition of some being who has benefited us: and equally clear that this being is implicitly recognized to be personal in nature. It is impossible to be grateful without being grateful *to* somebody—and to *somebody* rather than to something. Katherine Mansfield, then, did believe in God in the bottom of her heart, however uncertain may have been her hold of Him 'with the top of her mind'. Several years ago I was present at a service which was conducted by a well-known humanist. It contained only one prayer, and that was very much like an ordinary liturgical prayer of thanksgiving except that each phrase, where we should ordinarily say 'We thank Thee, O God', was introduced rather by the words 'We are thankful'. The humanist thought that in making this change he was leaving God out, but in this the humanist was wrong. Had he merely said 'We rejoice', he would indeed have left God out, but in saying 'We are thankful' he was unknowingly acknowledging His presence. To such a one, therefore, though it is impossible to prove that God exists, it is possible to prove that he already believes in Him—and believes in Him with such a belief as no mere proof could ever engender.

Mr. Aldous Huxley has somewhere observed that 'the course of every intellectual, if he pursues his journey long and unflinchingly enough, ends in the obvious from which the non-intellectuals have never stirred'. Yet if it be true (quoting Cook Wilson's phrase once again) that the proper business of philosophy is not to create belief but to bring it 'to a consciousness of itself', there is nothing essentially disappointing in this conclusion. It is only what Bacon said long ago: 'Depth in philosophy bringeth men's minds about to religion.'[1]

There are, moreover, several further reaches into which the same argument may be carried. For if it be true that all moral knowledge is in the last resort a fruit of the vision of God, then it must be possible to remount in thought to the reality of that vision from each and all of our moral conceptions. A notable example would be the conception of personality. Humanism has tended to regard personality as an essentially human attribute which we observe as actualized in ourselves and our neighbours, thus leaving theology with the task of so extending and refining the conception as to make it applicable to God. This task, however, has proved a desperate one; for how shall we make applicable to the Infinite a character which we began by regarding as the very headmark of the finite? What we have now come to see is that personality is not in the first instance something which we find in man, but something which we find somewhere else and desiderate for him. In other words, personality is like all true moral conceptions in

[1] *Essays*, xvi.

that it is not *a posteriori* but *a priori*, describing not the actual but the ideal. Judged by this ideal, some men have indeed more personality than others; yet the psychologists have made us realize afresh how little unified and integrated our human personalities are even at their best. Where then do we discover this ideal of personality against which we measure our human selfhood and find it so sadly wanting? Not, certainly, in an impersonal realm of *a priori* moral essences, as some would have us believe; for how can personality be found in the impersonal? The answer can only be that we find it in God; and we have already seen that such a revelation of God as personal is given in our every awareness of an unconditional moral demand. He who knows the poverty of his own personality knows it only because there has first been revealed to him the perfect personality of God. Professor Webb has shown how support for this view of the matter may be found in the fact that in the actual history of European thought and language the conception of personality was first framed to express something which men found in the nature of the Triune God, and only at a later date was drawn into the service of human psychology.[1]

What is true of personality is true also of goodness, as well as of such conceptions as infinity, eternity, omniscience, and omnipotence. All these conceptions we do certainly possess, yet it is clear that we do not find them in ourselves or anywhere in the created world. Rather do we and all creation stand condemned by being brought

[1] *God and Personality*, p. 20.

into the light of them. It must be then that we have some direct knowledge of Another who is Uncreated and in whom these qualities inhere. Such qualities are known, not *a posteriori* but *a priori*; which is to say, being interpreted, that they are first seen not on earth but in heaven. They are the names of the attributes which we find in God.

We have already seen how Thomism, in thinking it necessary to deny our possession of any direct knowledge of God, is faced by the alternative of demonstrating that such knowledge of the divine attributes as we do undoubtedly possess has been obtained by analogical reasoning from the attributes of man. Since I have already summarized St. Thomas's own version of this doctrine of the *analogia entis* in an earlier chapter, I shall content myself here with setting down some words said in defence of it by a modern Thomist to whose writings I have already more than once referred. 'The idea we have of a supremely perfect being', writes Dr. Hubert Box, 'is formed synthetically, that is, we form it by apprehending the various perfections in finite beings, excluding from them all limitations and imperfections, and conceiving them united in one being.' 'We maintain that our idea of the Infinite does not originate in direct intuition, but is reached in a negativo-positive way. The fact that the concept expresses its object, not in a purely positive manner, but by means of a negation, shows that it is the thought of the finite rather than the thought of the Infinite that is most natural to the human mind. We do not agree with those who assert that the idea of the

Infinite is a purely negative concept. But we hold that the positive perfections of creatures which we attribute to God are directly known to us only as accompanied by limitations. First of all, we think of created perfections as they exist in finite beings. We become aware of the limitations that attach to these perfections, by comparing less perfect finite beings with more perfect. We arrive at the idea of the Infinite by thinking of all conceivable perfections united in one Being, and excluding all the limitations which attend their realization in finite beings.' And so again of personality. 'Without doubt our conception of personality is mainly determined by an analysis of what constitutes *human* personality. . . . When we attribute personality to the Supreme Being, we attribute it only in an analogical and supereminent way.'[1]

Such a position seems to me quite impossible to maintain. To say that we gain the conception of perfect being by 'comparing less perfect beings with more perfect' is to forget that such a comparison cannot itself be instituted save by the aid of an already apprehended standard of perfection. How can we say that this is more perfect than that, unless we already know what perfection is? Surely there can be no reason for the adoption of so difficult a view apart from the prior refusal to contemplate the possibility of a direct knowledge of God. It is greatly to be deplored that the Roman Catholic thought

[1] Op. cit., pp. 130, 47 f., 205. Cf. also E. Gilson, *The Philosophy of St. Thomas Aquinas*, pp. 108–28; Erich Przywara, *Religionsphilosophie katholischer Theologie* (1916, English translation entitled *Polarity*), Part II; and the same author's later book, *Analogia Entis* (1932).

of our own day, by regarding itself as committed to the defence of St. Thomas's position in this matter, is (while thinking to protect itself, as it no doubt successfully does, against the worst) at the same time shutting itself out from the very best of post-Renaissance thought. What is true in the doctrine of the *analogia entis* is that the know-ledge of God does not precede our knowledge of man in time but is given 'in, with and under' such knowledge, and that therefore no one of God's attributes is ever given to us save in conjunction with—that is, in comparison with and in contrast to—some corresponding attribute of man. What is false is the assumption that the com-parison moves from man to God instead of from God to man. Such a view, if consistently carried out, is bound to end in anthropomorphism, that is, in a breach of the second commandment. We saw at the beginning of the foregoing chapter that if only the true insight of the two greatest post-Renaissance philosophies, namely the Cartesian and the Kantian, can be disengaged from their seriously aberrant tendencies, there is in them both a most valuable protection against such anthropomorphism, and therefore a real advance upon the Thomist teaching. In formulating what has usually been regarded as a new version of the ontological argument Descartes is going behind the tradition of St. Thomas to that of St. Anselm. 'Among the ideas I find in myself', he writes in the third of his *Meditations*, 'besides that which represents myself to myself, which here gives rise to no difficulty, there is another which represents a God; others that represent corporeal and inanimate things; others angels; others animals; and others again that represent men like myself. But as regards the ideas that represent other men, or animals, or angels, I can easily conceive their having been formed by the mingling and compounding of the other ideas which I have of corporeal things and of God, even if apart from myself there had existed in the world neither other men nor animals nor angels. And as regards the ideas of corporeal things, I never found in them anything so great or so excellent that I could not conceive it coming from myself. . . . Thus there remains only the single idea of God, in which I must consider whether there is anything that could not have come from myself. By the name of God I understand a substance infinite, eternal, immutable, independent, omniscient, omnipotent, and by which I myself and all the other things that exist (if in truth anything else exists) were created. But these qualities are so great and so elevated that the more attentively I consider them the less am I able to persuade myself that I could have derived their origin from myself alone. And hence it must necessarily be concluded, from all that I have already said, that God exists; for although the idea of substance is within me in virtue of my being myself a substance, I should nevertheless not have the idea of an infinite substance, I myself being only a finite being, if it had not been put in me by some substance that is veritably infinite.' It seems to me that, properly regarded, this is not a proof of the existence of God so much as a proof of the fact that we already believe in Him. What it confessedly does is not to give me a new idea but to clarify my understanding of an idea I already have, and of the nature of a conviction which I already implicitly possess. It is at all events a direct refutation of Dr. Box's statement that 'the idea we have of a supremely perfect being is formed synthetically'.

In the same way Kant's defence of the *a priori* against empiricism is to be regarded as essentially a defence of the second commandment against anthropomorphism. He does indeed argue that our ethical ideal is our clue to the nature of God, and we have criticized him for thus speaking as if the ideal were first apprehended as a self-subsistent essence which only afterwards found concreteness in a divine Person. But his whole philosophy is directed against the view that the clue to the ideal itself is given in the observed attributes of human nature. 'It is', he writes in the Preface to his *Grundlegung zur Metaphysik der Sitten*, 'of the utmost necessity to work out a pure moral philosophy which shall be entirely cleansed of all that is merely empirical and that belongs to anthropology; for that such a moral philosophy can exist appears at once from the common idea of duty and of the moral laws. Everybody must admit that if a law is to be morally binding, i.e. be the basis of an obligation, it must carry with it absolute necessity; . . . that accordingly the basis of obligation must not in this case be sought in human nature or in the external circumstances wherein man is placed, but only *a priori* in the conceptions of pure reason. . . . Thus not only do moral laws and principles differ in their very essence from all practical knowledge in which there is anything empirical, but all moral philosophy rests entirely on its pure part and, when applied to man, does not borrow the least thing from the knowledge of man, that is, from anthropology, but gives *a priori* laws to him as a rational being.' If then we are allowed to take seriously Kant's later willingness, apparent in the *Opus Postumum*, to believe that in the challenge of the moral law God Himself is already present to us, we may understand Kantianism to mean that, so far from human goodness (where it exists) providing our only clue to what God is, we must rather regard the divine Perfection as providing our only clue to what man should be. 'Be ye therefore perfect, even as your Father which is in heaven is perfect.'[1]

The case as regards the other attributes of God has been most clearly stated by Professor Kemp Smith. 'In respect of each and all of the ontological attributes', he writes, 'the Divine is not known through analogy with the self, or with any other creaturely mode of existence. These divine attributes *presuppose* God's existence, and save in this reference even their bare possibility cannot be established. If without any antecedent or independent apprehension of the Divine, we have to start from the creaturely, as exhibited in Nature and in man, and by way of inference and of analogy—on the pattern of what is found in the creaturely—through enlargement or other processes of ideal completion, to construct for ourselves concepts of the Divine, then the sceptics have been in the right; the attempt is an impossible one, condemned to failure from the start. We cannot reach the Divine merely by way of inference, not even if the inference

[1] Matthew v. 48.

be analogical in character. By no idealization of the creaturely can we transcend the creaturely.'[1]

With reference to each of these ontological predicates, infinity, eternity, immutability, omnipotence, omniscience, impassibility, and the rest, it may therefore be shown that they are all first discovered by us in the divine Reality that confronts us, and only then set in contrast to our finite, temporal, changeable, weak, ignorant, and suffering selves, first to our own exceeding humiliation but afterwards to our very great rejoicing. But it is unnecessary to carry the argument further in this place. We have said enough to make it plain that the spiritual life of man is, in every part and mode of it, a derived and dependent life; and that, like to those physical bodies about which we learned in our schoolbooks that their centre of gravity falls outside their own periphery, so also man is a being whose centre lies not in himself but in God. 'O Lord,' exclaimed Jeremiah, 'I know that the way of man is not in himself.'[2] Even the most elementary and familiar of our spiritual experiences are robbed of their true meaning if they be regarded otherwise than as part of the soul's dealings with One who all our lives through is seeking us out in love—

> What are they but vaunt-couriers
> To lead you to His sight?
> What are they but the effluence
> Of uncreated light?[3]

[1] Op. cit., p. 13 f. [2] Jeremiah x. 23.
[3] Joseph the Hymnographer as paraphrased by J. M. Neale.

INDEX

Aaron, 118.
Abihu, 118.
Acts of the Apostles, the, 180.
Adickes, E., 131.
Addressability, 29.
Alexander, S., 202, 211.
Ambrose, St., 126.
Anabaptism, 70, 86–8.
Analogia entis, vide Analogy, Method of.
Analogy, Method of, 110 f., 204–7, 252–8.
Animism, 215.
Anknüpfungspunkt, 19 ff., 25 ff.
Anselm, St., 3, 117, 170, 171, 254, § 12 *passim*.
Anthropomorphism, 254–7
Apologetics, 14 f.
Aquinas, St. Thomas, 84 f., 126, 127, 129, 132, 141, 142, 149, 151, 167–72, 179, 193–7, 204, 206, 230–5, 252, 254, § 9 *passim*.
Argument from design, 124, 126.
Aristotelians, 149, 167 f.
Aristotle, 108, 111, 138, 167 f.
Arnold, Matthew, 90.
Arunta, 79.
Atheism, 4–7, 119–21, 244, §§ 5–6 *passim*.
Attributes of God, 251–8.
Auber, Harriet, 234.
Augustine, St., 25, 57, 81, 88, 117, 195 f.
Autonomy of the will, 245–8.

Bacon, Francis, 47, 61, 114, 250.
Baillie, D. M., 69 n., 114 n.
Baptism, sacrament of, 86–8.
Barth, Karl, 15, 17–35, 98–101, 130, 165, 187–9, 193, 196 n., 203, 219 f., 224, 225, 228, 235 f., 237.
Beaumont, M. de, 185.

Berdyaev, N., 42.
Bergson, H., 162.
Berkeley, Bishop, 133, 148, 151, 205 f.
Bernard of Clairvaux, St., 170.
Bonaventure, St., 132, 170–2, 173, 197.
Bonhoeffer, D., 70 n.
Bowman, A. A., 202, 217, 220, 224, 245 n.
Box, H., 174 f., 206, 252 f., 256.
Brethren of Charity, 172.
Briggs, C. A., 120.
Browning, R., 240 n.
Brunner, Emil, 24 n., 28–35, 42, 69, 98–101, 164, 181, 228.
Buber, Martin, 79 n., 161, 203, 208 f., 213 n., 217, 221–4, 226 n., 236.
Buchman, Frank, 15.
Burgh, W. G. de, 202, 226, 234 n.

Cairns, D. S., 18 n., 229.
Calvin, 20, 27, 55, 78 n., 87, 231–3.
Campbell, C. A., 233 n.
Categorical imperative, 243–5, 256 f.
Catherine of Genoa, St., 34 n.
Childish experience, 3–5, 181–4, 209.
Children, the spiritual status of, 71 f., 86–9.
Cicero, 6 f.
Claudel, P., 246.
Clemens, Titus Flavius, 49.
Coates, A., 217 n., 220.
Codrington, R. H., 79.
Coffin, H. S., 119.
Collingwood, R. G., 65, 103, 139–41.
Communism, 50.
Confirmation, 86–8.
Conversion, § 8 *passim*.

259